The
Kingdom
of Shalom Books

"For the earth shall be filled with the knowledge of the glory of the LORD, as the waters cover the sea." ~ Habakkuk 2:14 KJV

THE LANGUAGE
OF GOD YAHWEH

ת TO א
SPIRITUAL, MYSTICAL HEBREW

The
Kingdom of Shalom

A Guide To The Inner Meanings Of Aleph-Beth

KOS Books
KOS Publishing
www.kingdomofshalom.com
info@kingdomofshalom.com

Your support of the author's rights is appreciated.
"The Language of God Yahweh
Aleph to Tav - Spiritual, Mystical Hebrew"
Printed in the United States of America
ISBN: 979-8-9896094-2-0 Paperback Version
eBook Version Available on the Website and online

Editorial: KOS Editorial Team
Editing: Olivia Jayden and Toni Lieght
Cover Images: Cre8tive Minds
Cover Design: Tyron Roshantha
Content Editing: Cre8tive Minds
Layout: Shams

Kingdom

Table of **Contents**

THE STORY BEHIND THIS BOOK

This book is the culmination of over 25 years of devoted study and teaching of the Hebrew letters, an odyssey through the sacred language of God, Yahweh, which we affectionately refer to as the Aleph-Beth. Throughout these years, I have had the privilege of guiding many eager minds, both young and old, on their journey to discover and master this divine language.

The lessons taught and insights gained from both my students and teachers have been carefully integrated into the intricate fabric of this work. The exchanges with those who are gaining knowledge from me, and notably those who are imparting knowledge to me, have had a profound transformative effect. The purpose of this book is to act as a repository of knowledge and to serve as a bridge that links readers to the profound spiritual essence of Aleph-Beth.

It is my heartfelt intention that this book serves as a gateway for seekers to glimpse the profound mysteries embedded within these ancient characters. More than just learning to remember and study, I invite you to embark on your own personal discovery of the Aleph-Beth, exploring its divine nuances and how they resonate through the fabric of spirituality and truth.

KINGDOM OF
SHALOM WORKS

The Kingdom of Shalom emerged from a pursuit to inspire and support those on a spiritual journey and a desire for moral actions to speak louder than words. It is evolving into the Great Work that הוהי YHWH (Yahweh) called for it to become. It is proof that when הוהי YHWH (Yahweh) calls, you must answer.

As an organization, we are driven by spiritual ideas, bold actions, and a strong moral foundation of support. We are bringing the Spiritual (the Kingdom) down into the minds and hearts of the people.

"Behold, I will do a new thing; now it shall
spring forth; shall ye not know it?
I will even make a way in the wilderness, and
rivers in the desert."
-Isaiah 43:19 KJV

Visit the Kingdom of Shalom for more KOS Books, Art and Designs, Clothing, and other works.

The
Kingdom
of Shalom

DEDICATION

This book is dedicated to the spiritual resurrection of the righteous people of the Earth, the release and construct of Spirit and Truth, and the complete establishment of the Kingdom of God, יהוה *(YHWH) YAHWEH*

--- The Kingdom of Shalom. ---

PREFACE

Welcome to a journey through Aleph to Tav, a path that explores the profound depths and the divine essence of the Hebrew alphabet. This book is more than a linguistic guide. It is an invitation to traverse the sacred landscape of a language that has shaped the spiritual and cultural heritage of countless generations. Here, each letter holds a world of meaning, each mark tells a story, and every word is a bridge connecting the earthly to the divine. As you embark on this journey, you will learn to recognize and pronounce each letter and also delve into the rich tapestry of history and spirituality that these letters weave.

The Hebrew language, referred to as the Aleph-Beth, is celebrated as the "Language of God Yahweh." According to tradition, it was with these letters that the universe was crafted, each character a divine tool wielded during the act of creation. This ancient script is a means of communication and a series of sacred symbols, each resonating with cosmic energy. As we dive into these letters, we interact with a tradition that perceives the letters of this language as living entities that possess the power to shape reality.

From the mystical "Let There Be Light," which in the Hebrew tradition refers to spiritual enlightenment, to the fundamental belief that these letters are the building blocks of the universe, the Hebrew alphabet offers a unique window into the spiritual ethos of the Israelite people and the broader human quest for understanding.

In the chapters that follow, we will trace the evolution of these ancient characters from their earliest forms inscribed on stone to their current iterations bound in modern texts. This historical voyage is punctuated by key archaeological discoveries, from ancient scrolls to inscribed artifacts that offer us tangible links to the past. Through these relics, we gain insight into the practical functions of Hebrew and its enduring significance as a vehicle for cultural and spiritual expression.

As languages evolved, Hebrew also adapted to the diasporas and demands of its speakers. However, in this book, we do not explore how Hebrew flourished into a dynamic and modern language. Instead, our focus is directed toward its ancient and spiritual origins as the living language of God Yahweh. Each phase of the letter's potency reflects broader context, mysteries, historical currents, and the unyielding spirit of a language that refused to be relegated to the archives of history.

Unlocking
Mystical Gates:
The Multifaceted Hebrew Letters

Beyond its sounds and shapes, each Hebrew letter is a complex entity, representing numbers, words, and profound spiritual symbols. This book journeys into the mystical dimensions of the Aleph-Beth, where letters serve as portals to deeper wisdom and spiritual truths. Through the insights of legendary scholars and mystics, from ancient texts like the Zohar to modern interpretations, we uncover the layers of meaning that each letter holds.

As you turn these pages, you are invited to embark on a transformative journey, a voyage that transcends time and space, bridging the past with the present, the sacred with the profane. Whether you are a student of language, a seeker of wisdom, or a connoisseur of history, this guide promises to enrich your understanding of Hebrew and, in doing so, deepen your connection to the divine.

Brace yourself for a journey into the Aleph to Tav, letters formed by lines and curves, yet vibrant vessels holding immense historical, spiritual, and cosmic significance. Let's embark on this journey together and may the knowledge and understanding you gain light your way.

While intended for beginners, readers traveling through **"Aleph to Tav"** are exposed to more than an alphabet. They explore a sacred tradition that sees the Hebrew letters as a medium through which the world was created and continues to be sustained. Learning these letters is an invitation to take part in a millennia-old tradition of inquiry into the nature of language, spirituality, and existence itself. As we explore the aleph-beth, we will immerse ourselves in the world of those who first wrote these letters on parchment, stone, and clay, using them to convey their thoughts, laws, history, and spiritual visions.

The Hebrew Aleph-Beth chart is a profound system of symbols that goes beyond mere letters of the alphabet. Each letter holds deep mystical and spiritual significance. Unlike the English alphabet, the Hebrew letters are considered to embody divine energies and carry meanings that extend into numerology, linguistics, and sacred teachings. The Hebrew Aleph-Beth is read from right to left, beginning with the first character, Aleph, which represents unity and the divine source. Following Aleph, each subsequent letter adds layers of meaning and insight, creating a holistic system where language and spirituality are intricately linked. This ancient script serves as a bridge between the earthly and the divine, offering profound insights into the nature of reality and existence.

INTRODUCTION

The Divine Language of Yahweh the Aleph-Beth

The Hebrew Letters as the Language of God Yahweh

The Hebrew alphabet, known as Aleph-Beth, is regarded not merely as a collection of arbitrary symbols but as the divine language used by God, Yahweh, to manifest the universe. Each letter serves as a sacred vessel that channels divine energy, making these characters far more than mere linguistic tools—they are the very essence of creation itself.

What is the Divine Essence of Aleph-Beth? Well, in ancient mystical Israelite traditions, it is believed that the universe was spoken into existence by Yahweh through the power of the Hebrew letters. Each letter is infused with divine life, acting as a conduit for Yahweh's creative energy. This sacred text, beginning with "Let there be light," where light symbolizes light as spiritual illumination, underscores the profound role of Aleph-Beth in enlightening the human soul. Spiritual illumination refers to the profound realization and understanding of divine truths, transcending ordinary knowledge and perception. This realization and understanding comes from Aleph-Beth.

Each Hebrew letter is also traditionally associated with a specific angel, serving as a fundamental component of the celestial machinery. These angels are considered guardians of the cosmic order. Each is imbued with the task of guiding and directing the spiritual forces that flow through the universe. The letters, therefore, are seen as living, breathing entities that maintain the balance of all existence.

The idea that Hebrew letters make up the fundamental elements of creation coincides with the understanding that the universe comprises vibrations or energy patterns. Similar to how particles in physics vibrate to manifest physical reality, the Hebrew letters vibrate spiritually to create and sustain all life forms and matter. These letters sculpt the fabric of reality, shaping it through divine decree and the profound spiritual forces they command.

Understanding and engaging with the Hebrew letters leads to a path of spiritual illumination. Each letter offers unique insights into the divine blueprint of the universe, facilitating a deeper connection with God Yahweh and the sacred mysteries of existence. The study of Aleph-Beth is thus a transformative journey in gaining knowledge and evolving spiritually, aiming to align one's soul with the Divine Will of God Yahweh.

Historical Echoes of the Hebrew Letters

The Hebrew Letters hold a storied history woven deeply into the fabric of ancient civilizations and religious texts. Its evolution from ancient to modern forms tells a tale of cultural interchange, religious significance, and linguistic development.

The Hebrew language is an ancient tongue with roots stretching back over three thousand years. It emerged from the Canaanite branch of languages, which were themselves offshoots of Semitic, a language family originating in the Middle East. This family includes Hebrew, Aramaic, Phoenician, and the more distantly related Chaldean. As you learn the Hebrew letters, you are also glimpsing into the linguistic framework that shaped much of the ancient Near East.

The origins of the Hebrew alphabet can be traced back to the Proto-Canaanite and Phoenician scripts around the 12th to 10th centuries BCE. These early alphabetic systems gradually morphed into the Paleo-Hebrew script, which directly influenced the form of the letters used in the earliest biblical manuscripts. This script was used during the period of the Kingdoms of Israel and Judah, making it a contemporary witness to the events narrated in the Hebrew Bible.

In looking at Hebrew letters, you find they are more than tools for writing. These characters are imbued with profound spiritual significance. Each letter's shape and sound were believed to hold divine influence, reflecting the mystical belief that language is a gift from God Yahweh. This connection is clear in the Book of Genesis, where Yahweh uses words to create the heavens and the earth, showcasing the power of Aleph-Beth as the fundamental building blocks of the universe.

Discoveries: Significant archaeological findings have provided tangible links to the ancient usage of Hebrew letters. Inscriptions found on ancient stones, pottery, and scrolls offer critical insights into the early forms of Hebrew script. For instance, the Gezer Calendar, an ancient agricultural almanac, uses ancient Hebrew script to detail monthly activities, demonstrating the practical application of writing in daily life. The Dead Sea Scrolls, which contain some of the oldest known biblical manuscripts, feature both the ancient and more developed forms of Hebrew, illustrating the script's evolution over the centuries.

These artifacts underscore Hebrew's ancient and continued endurance. They enhance our understanding of the historical contexts in which these letters were used. They also provide a direct link to the past, offering a glimpse into the daily lives, spiritual practices, and communal structures of ancient Hebrew-speaking communities.

Throughout history, scholars and theologians have studied the Hebrew letters to uncover deeper meanings within the biblical texts. Figures like the philosopher Philo of Alexandria, a Hellenistic Jewish philosopher who lived in Alexandria, in the Roman province of Egypt, and later Kabbalistic scholars interpreted these letters as cosmic codes containing hidden wisdom about the divine nature of the universe. These interpretations often explore the numerical values of letters (called gematria), which uncover layered meanings in scriptural verses that go beyond the surface narrative.

The connection of the Hebrew letters to biblical texts is historical and linguistic but profoundly spiritual. Each letter is seen as a channel of divine energy with the power to influence the material world, echoing the biblical concept that Yahweh spoke the world into existence through these sacred characters.

The Evolution of Hebrew Through the Ages

The journey of the Hebrew language, from its ancient origins to its modern form, is a story of resilience, adaptation, and revival. Over the centuries, Hebrew has undergone significant transformations, adapting to the needs of its speakers while preserving its deep spiritual and cultural roots.

The ancient Hebrew script used during the biblical era gradually evolved into the Aramaic script after the Babylonian exile—this script is known as the Imperial Aramaic script. The Imperial Aramaic script refers to the writing system used across the Persian Empire, which standardized Aramaic as the official language and script for administration and communication. Aramaic was already widely used in the Near East before the rise of the Persian Empire. Still, it was under the Persians, specifically from the time of Darius I (522-486 BCE) onwards, that this script was formalized and promoted as the empire-wide standard for official correspondence.

After returning from the Babylonian exile, the Israelites - Judeans, under leaders like Zerubbabel, Ezra, and Nehemiah, were actively rebuilding their community and spiritual practices in Jerusalem. During this period, they adopted the Aramaic language. However, Hebrew remained the language of spiritual and sacred literature.

The widespread use of Aramaic among the Israelites under Persian rule wasn't because of an official decree or formal policy. Instead, it was a natural and practical response to the circumstances at the time. Under Persian rule, Aramaic was already established for administration and governance across the vast Persian Empire, which included diverse peoples and languages. Because Aramaic was the dominant administrative and cultural language, it was practical and almost necessary for the Israelites and other subjugated peoples to adopt it for their own administrative, daily communications, and even cultural exchanges.

Aramaic language comes from Aram, the son of Shem and grandson of Noah. Aramaic was the lingua franca of the time. Lingua franca is a term that originally referred to a mixed language used for communication between traders in the Mediterranean. By using Aramaic, the Israelite community could effectively interact with the Persian authorities and other communities within the empire, facilitating smoother governance, trade, legal matters, and cultural integration. This pragmatic adoption ensured that the Israelite people remained effectively integrated and operative within the socio-political framework of the Persian Empire. The use of Aramaic and its script naturally permeated life and documents from this period, including parts of the biblical books of Daniel and Ezra, which are written in Aramaic.

Over time, this led to the development of the Square Hebrew script, which is still used in modern times. The transition involved a transformation in form and symbolized a broader cultural and linguistic shift influenced and shaped by geopolitical changes. The transition from the Paleo-Hebrew script to the Aramaic-derived square script (the form of the Hebrew alphabet used today) was gradual and influenced by these historical and socio-political contexts.

The use of this script was later standardized for writing Hebrew, which continued into the period of the Masoretes, who were active many centuries later, around the 6th to 10th centuries CE. Some suggest that the Masoretes were primarily Karaites, while others believe they were not. They are known as the Jewish scribes who worked to preserve the Hebrew Bible's original text. The Masoretes added vowel points and cantillation marks to the original consonants to show how words should be pronounced. They also added notes, called Masorah, to explain textual issues and prevent changes.

The Hebrew language underwent a significant transformation during the late 19th and early 20th centuries, resulting in its revival as a spoken language. Eliezer Ben-Yehuda played a crucial role in the language's revival as it exists today. He created new words and adapted old ones to suit modern needs, effectively transforming Hebrew into a language capable of carrying out the daily realities of life in the modern world.

Unlocking the Secrets of the Aleph-Beth

Again, in this book, we will look at the Hebrew letters from an ancient viewpoint as the language of God Yahweh. Looking at the Aleph-Beth this way deepens your knowledge of these ancient multifaceted Hebrew letters. It all starts with grasping the concepts and secrets of the alphabet.

Ancient Hebrew existed of consonants only. Writing systems that use only consonants can convey a wide range of words with fewer characters. This type of writing system can lead to a highly efficient and flexible script, which is adaptable to multiple dialects or languages. While these writing systems have similar consonantal roots, their vowel sounds differ. This flexibility was useful in Semitic languages, where word roots based on consonants carry the core meaning, and vowels adjust the tense, gender, or number.

The consonant-only script reflects the strong oral tradition in ancient Hebrew culture. Knowledge of the correct pronunciation and meaning of words was preserved and transmitted orally. Proficiency in Hebrew letters was necessary to reinforce this culture that was deeply rooted in memorization, oral recitation, and communal learning. The reliance on oral tradition to complement the written text ensured that language and scripture, the living entities, were constantly engaged with and discussed within the community.

From a spiritual perspective, the consonant-only nature of Hebrew is profound because it aligns with mystical beliefs about the nature of language and creation. The text of the Bible is a narrative, but it is also a sequence of divine commands and actions. Eliminating vowels introduces a profound and mysterious quality to the text, implying veiled messages and profound insights that unfold through scholarly examination and divine revelation.

Exploring the Aleph-Beth is an educational endeavor that is a profound journey into spiritual and intellectual awakening. As you engage with these ancient letters, allow them to expand your knowledge and mind. Each letter invites you into a dynamic interaction with the language and traditions of Yahweh. Studying them is not a passive absorption of facts. It is an active, vibrant pursuit that challenges your mind and spirit. As you learn the intricacies of each letter and uncover the layers of meaning they hold, you take part in a tradition of deep contemplation and dialogue that has enriched minds for centuries.

Active engagement with each letter brings you closer to the essence of the Hebrew language. Studying the letters brings you into a fuller connection with your spirit and with Yahweh, fostering a sense of oneness and understanding that transcends the written word.

An Overview of the Hebrew Aleph-Beth

Aleph-Beth, also known as the Hebrew language, comprises 22 letters with deep historical, numerical, and mystical meanings. The letters have their roots in the Proto-Canaanite script and developed into the Phoenician script, which influenced both the Hebrew and Latin alphabets.

In addition to the 22 letters, there are five special and specific forms known as **"final letters"** or **"Sofit forms."** These forms are exclusive to the letters Kaph, Mem, Nun, Peh, and Tzaddi. They show up at the end of a word. These final forms are stylistic variations but hold distinct roles and meanings within various contexts of Hebrew writing.

How to Use This Book

This book has been crafted to serve as both a guidebook and a workbook, ensuring it will accompany you throughout your Aleph-Beth journey. Each letter is accompanied by in-depth explanations that examine its form, numerical value, and profound mystical connotations. To fully benefit from this book, it is recommended that you actively engage with the content in multiple ways.

1. **Highlight Key Information:** As you read through each letter's description, highlight the facts and insights that stand out to you. Highlighting will help you quickly locate significant information when you review the material.

2. **Take Detailed Notes:** Write your thoughts, reflections, and any additional insights that come to mind as you study each letter. These notes will personalize your learning experience and serve as a valuable reference as you continue to explore the Hebrew letters.

3. **Study at Your Own Pace:** Whether it takes a day or a week, focus on fully understanding each letter before moving on to the next. This deliberate pace ensures that you deeply comprehend the multi-layered meanings of each letter, enriching your overall grasp of the Hebrew language.

4. **Review and Reflect:** As you progress, regularly review your highlighted sections and notes. This ongoing reflection will reinforce your learning and help you integrate Aleph-Beth's spiritual and linguistic wisdom into your daily life.

Upon completing this book, you will have created a personalized and annotated guide to the Hebrew letters. By using this customized tool, you will enhance your understanding of each letter and also have a lasting resource to support your continued study and exploration of the Hebrew language and its mystical traditions.

By approaching this book as a structured yet personal study journey, you will unlock the profound wisdom encoded within the Hebrew Aleph-Beth, drawing closer to the spiritual heritage that these letters embody.

Aleph-Beth Overview Reference Guide:
Full Hebrew Aleph-Bet Table

Hebrew Letter	Name	Transliteration	Numeric Value	English Equivalent	Pictorial Representation
א	Aleph	Alef	1	A	(an ox's head)
ב	Beth	Bet	2	B	(a tent, house)
ג	Gimel	Gimel	3	G	(a camel)
ד	Dalet	Dalet	4	D	(a door, tent door)
ה	Heh	He	5	H	(window, man with arms raised)
ו	Wav	Vav	6	V	(a nail, hook)
ז	Zayin	Zayin	7	Z	(a weapon, crown)
ח	Cheth	Chet	8	H	(life force, a wall)
ט	Teth	Tet	9	T	(a basket)
י	Yod	Yod	10	Y	(arm and closed hand or fist)
ך כ	Kaph	Kaph	20	K	(an open palm)
ל	Lamed	Lamed	30	L	(an ox goad)
ם מ	Mem	Mem	40	M	(water, womb)
ן נ	Nun	Nun	50	N	(fish, seed)
ס	Samekh	Samekh	60	S	(a support, construct form, thorn)
ע	Ayin	Ayin	70	None	(an eye)
ף פ	Peh	Pe	80	P	(a mouth)
ץ צ	Tzaddi	Tzaddi	90	TS	(a righteous one, hook, fishhook)
ק	Qoph	Qoph	100	Q	(eye of a needle, to surround)
ר	Resh	Resh	200	R	(head, beginning, face)
ש	Shin	Shin	300	SH	(tooth, front teeth)
ת	Tav	Tav	400	T	(a mark, sign, code)

Now, as we turn the page to explore the first letter, Aleph, we embark on a profound journey to connect with the language of God Yahweh, the angels, and the very act of creation. The Bible teaches us that God Yahweh is a spirit and that understanding Him requires us to engage with the spiritual dimensions of our existence. Each Hebrew letter is a gateway to this spiritual understanding, offering keys to unlocking the deeper spiritual aspects of our being.

Aleph invites you to begin this sacred encounter, opening your mind and spirit to the divine communications inscribed in the universe. As you study Aleph and each letter after that, you are absorbing a spiritual practice that connects you to a tradition that has shaped history and encoded the spiritual wisdom of the ages into its very letters.

Prepare to be transformed as these letters reveal insights into divine knowledge and foster a deeper connection with the spiritual forces that permeate our world. Your study of this book is not just an educational pursuit; it is a spiritual voyage that promises to enlighten your understanding of the universe and your place within it.

Let's begin our exploration from Aleph to Tav, discovering each letter as a world unto itself.

אבגדההוז

חטיכלמנ

סעפצקר

שת

CHAPTER 1

Aleph:
The Silent Leader

Aleph (א)
Modern Hebrew Letter
Modern Aleph as used in contemporary Hebrew

Ancient Pictorial/Glyph: (an ox head)
The ox head is the ancient representation of Aleph,
symbolizing strength and leadership.

Introduction to Aleph

Welcome to your first step into the Hebrew aleph-bet: Aleph. As the **1st letter, Aleph** holds a distinguished position, being both the silent harbinger of speech and a sign deeply rooted in ancient symbolism. This letter is the starting point of the Aleph-Beth's order. But it also invites you to embark on a captivating journey through Hebrew's mystical and historical realms.

Name and Spellings

Aleph is also spelled Alef, Eleph, and Alif. It serves as a portal to the past. As we explore its various forms of aleph and other letters, remember that each spelling carries its own meaning that echoes a time preserved through the continuity of writing.

Pronunciation Guide

Pronounced 'ah-lef,' Aleph might remind you of the **'a'** in **'father,'** which is the Hebrew word 'abba,' and the 'lef' is like a musical 'clef.' Although Aleph itself is silent, it often carries a breathy tone when paired with vowels, subtly influencing its sound without asserting its own.

Corresponding Greek and English Letters

Aleph corresponds to the Greek Alpha (A, α) and the English letter A.
Like its Greek and English counterparts, Aleph stands at the forefront, setting the stage for all letters that follow.

Numerical Value

In Hebrew numerology, known as Gematria, Aleph represents the number 1
The number one number signifies oneness, new beginnings, primacy, and the singularity of the universe—an apt symbol for the first letter of the alphabet. Aleph is also the number 1000, which shows its continued power.

Meaning of Aleph as Oneness, the Ox and Breath

As the first letter of the Hebrew Aleph-Beth, Aleph symbolizes oneness and unity, reflecting the singular essence of God Yahweh. To be one with Yahweh means to recognize and embrace the Divine presence within and around us, acknowledging that all creation emanates from a single, unified source.

Spiritually, oneness signifies a deep connection with the divine, where the boundaries between self and the Divine dissolve, leading to a profound sense of harmony and alignment with Yahweh's will. Mentally, oneness represents the integration of our thoughts, emotions, and actions with Divine Wisdom, fostering a state of inner peace, clarity, and purpose. Aleph teaches us that by attuning ourselves to this unity, we can transcend our limitations and experience a deeper, more meaningful existence in alignment with the infinite and eternal nature of Yahweh.

Aleph originally depicted the 'ox' or an ox head in ancient scripts, symbolizing strength and leadership. This representation, derived from its Proto-Sinaitic antecedent, evolved over centuries into the abstract forms seen in modern Hebrew script. The ox, a vital asset in ancient agricultural societies, was a symbol of both physical power and economic wealth.

Aleph also conveys the concept of 'breath'—the essence of life itself in many spiritual and philosophical contexts. This dual symbolism encapsulates the fundamental aspects of existence: the material and the spiritual, the visible and the invisible.

The Hebrew letter Aleph is also associated with the concept of a **"yoke."** This symbolism reflects the idea of connection and unity, as a yoke joins two entities together to work in harmony. Aleph, therefore, represents the divine principle that unites heaven and earth, the spiritual and the material. It embodies the potential and balance between opposing forces, guiding them towards a unified purpose.

Further deepening its mystique, the modern form of Aleph can be seen as comprising two Yods ('), one above and one below, connected by a diagonal Vav (ו). This formation is rich in symbolism. The Yods represent the divine sparks, or the essence of Yahweh's presence, at the top and bottom of the universe, suggesting that the divine encompasses all that is above and below. The Vav, connecting these two points, symbolizes the continuum of the spiritual and the earthly, acting as a conduit between heaven and earth. This structure is a bridge to both worlds, expressing unity and connection to all things.

Interesting Fact

Aleph represents the oneness of Yahweh. Its silent pronunciation suggests the ineffable, indescribable nature of the divine, underscoring its role in words like **'emet'** (truth) and **'ahava'** (love), highlighting its profound spiritual significance.

The Aleph is a symbol of humility. Although it is the first letter of the alphabet, Aleph doesn't appear at the beginning of the Hebrew Bible. This deliberate omission is viewed as a lesson in modesty, illustrating that true leadership is rooted in humility. Despite Aleph's foundational significance and its numerical value of 1, it steps aside to emphasize the importance of collective unity over individual prominence.

Spelling Aleph
(Aleph, Lamed, Peh)

"The Divine Source (**Aleph**) leads through Teaching (**Lamed**) and is revealed through Speech (**Peh**)."

The Hebrew spelling of Aleph

אלף

Aleph (א): Represents the Divine Source.

Lamed (ל): Symbolizes teaching and guidance.

Peh (ף): Reveals through speech and expression.

In this combination, Aleph embodies the powerful relationship between divine unity, teaching, and the creative potential of speech.

Chapter Engagement

Three-Minute Meditation for Aleph

1. **Find a Comfortable Position:** Sit comfortably in a chair or on the floor. Close your eyes and take a few deep breaths, inhaling through your nose and exhaling through your mouth.

2. **Visualize Aleph:** Imagine the letter Aleph in your mind. See its form as two Yods connected by a diagonal Vav. Visualize the letter glowing with divine light, radiating unity and oneness.

3. **Reflect on Unity:** Contemplate how Aleph symbolizes unity and the divine source of all creation. Think about how the letter connects higher realms (upper Yod) with the material world (lower Yod) through the diagonal Vav.

4. **Focus on Leadership:** Reflect on the concept of divine leadership embodied by Aleph. Consider how this unity leads to purposeful actions, guiding you toward your highest potential.

5. **Breathe and Connect:** With each breath, focus on the unity and leadership of Aleph. Feel how this ancient letter connects you to the broader universe and your unique purpose.

6. **Gradually Return:** Slowly open your eyes and return to the present. Carry the feeling of unity and leadership with you as you move forward.

CHAPTER 2

Beth:
The House of
Foundation

Beth (בּ)
Modern Hebrew Letter
The modern Beth is used in contemporary Hebrew.

Ancient Pictorial/Glyph: (a house)

House is the ancient representation of Beth,
symbolizing a temple, family, or dwelling place.

Introduction to Beth

Welcome to the second letter of the Hebrew aleph-bet: Beth. Representing the structure, plus both the concept of building and the concept of beginning, Beth serves as the foundational character from which narratives and edifices alike are constructed. It symbolizes the entry into the manifold aspects of existence.

Name and Spellings

Beth is also seen spelled as Bet, vet, and beis. It embodies the threshold to all stories and spaces. As we explore Beth, remember that each variation of its name opens the door to a rich linguistic heritage with roots deeply embedded in the beginnings of written language.

Pronunciation Guide

It is pronounced like 'bet' with a soft 'b' sound as in 'bed.' Beth is also pronounced as its dual 'vet' with a soft 'v' sound. This dual pronunciation capacity gives Beth a versatile role in Hebrew phonetics. For example, the Hebrew word for 'house' is 'bayith' (בַּיִת).

Corresponding Greek and English Letters

Beth corresponds to the Greek Beta (B, β) and the English letter B. Just as in Greek and English, Beth in Hebrew serves as a strong pillar, supporting the structure of words and meanings it constructs.

Numerical Value

Beth represents the number 2.

This number highlights the concept of duality and plurality, emphasizing the exceptional nature of One as the foundation of everything else. It symbolizes the beginning of duality, such as the inside and outside of a house, and emphasizes division and connection, making it the fundamental symbol for beginnings and relational dynamics.

Beth as the House and Symbol of Duality

Beth originally depicted a house, 'bayith' in ancient scripts, signifying shelter and domicile. This form harkens back to Beth's Proto-Canaanite and Phoenician origins, where it visually resembled a simple abode. As civilizations evolved, so did the portrayal of Beth, which now embodies more than just a house—it symbolizes any dwelling place for the body or spirit — the temple.

Beth symbolizes the house of God Yahweh, representing a dwelling place for the divine presence both within the universe and within us. As the house of Yahweh, Beth signifies a sacred space where the divine and the human meet, emphasizing the importance of creating and maintaining environments—physical, mental, and spiritual—where Yahweh's presence can be felt and honored. This concept extends beyond physical structures, reminding us that our hearts and minds are also temples where we can invite and cultivate a connection with Yahweh. By embodying the qualities of Beth, we open ourselves to the nurturing and protective aspects of the divine, creating a harmonious sanctuary within that reflects the sacred relationship between the Creator and creation.

Beth is composed of three vavs, reflecting the structural elements of a house. This design shows the roof, the floor, and one wall. It is open on one end. Bet symbolizes our dwelling place in the world of duality and illusion.

Beth's representation extends to metaphorical meanings as well, illustrating concepts of security, inclusivity, and foundational structures. Beth holds a pivotal role in many Hebrew words, such as 'Bereshit' (in the beginning), the very first word of the Torah, which sets the stage for the creation story. Beyond its architectural connotations, Beth represents otherness, the paradox of creation, and a dwelling place in the material world. It also embodies the duality of nature, including the male and female principles, symbolizing the comprehensive aspects of existence.

Interesting Fact

Beth is linked to the concept of duality and free will. As the second letter of the Hebrew alphabet, Beth symbolizes the separation between heaven and earth and the inherent choice humanity has to seek the divine. Beth is considered the point of union between finite and infinite, the physical and the spiritual, reflecting its role in the creation story, where the world was conceptualized from a divine point. Additionally, Beth's presence at the beginning of the Bible in the word **'Bereishit'** ('in the beginning') underscores its thematic importance as the starting point of Genesis and all creation narratives.

Beth is believed to be a symbol of the **'Birthing Place,'** representing the cosmic womb that nurtures creation. It is the first Hebrew letter with a sound, which aligns with the belief that the physical world is birthed from the spiritual. Beth is the cosmic container that receives and nurtures divine wisdom and sustains life. It is also the first letter in the word **'bracha'** (blessing), indicating that the house of Beth is where divine favor and abundance can flourish.

Spelling Beth

(Beth, Yod, Tav)

"The Dwelling (Beth) provides Spiritual Guidance (Yod) and is protected by the Covenant (Tav)."

The Hebrew spelling of Beth

ב י ת

Beth (ב): Represents a house or dwelling, symbolizing shelter and inclusivity.
Yod (י): Symbolizes spiritual guidance, the divine spark that resides within and animates the house.
Tav (ת): Signifies covenant, marking the dwelling as a place of sacred commitment and protection.
Together, these letters show that Beth embodies the sacred space where spiritual guidance is embraced, and divine commitment provides a protective boundary.

Chapter Engagement

Exploring Beth Building a Sacred Dwelling

1. **Visualize the Dwelling:** Close your eyes and take a few deep breaths to relax. Visualize the letter Beth as a house or shelter, welcoming you with open doors. Picture Beth offering protection, warmth, and inclusivity.

2. **Reflect on the Meaning:** Consider Beth's symbolism as a sacred dwelling. Reflect on how it represents the connection between the material and spiritual realms, a place where divine guidance **(Yod)** and commitment **(Tav)** are found.

3. **Create Your Space:** Take three minutes to imagine building a sacred space that reflects your values. Think about what you would include in this house: what makes it special and unique? How would you incorporate elements of spiritual guidance, kindness, and protection into this dwelling?

4. **Identify Real-Life Applications:** Open your eyes and identify ways to create this kind of welcoming, protective space in your daily life. How can you embody Beth's spirit through your actions and relationships?

5. **Write Down Your Insights:** Take a moment to write down your reflections, noting any new perspectives or practices that came to mind during this exercise.

CHAPTER 3

Gimel: The Journeying Camel

Gimel (ג)
Modern Hebrew Letter
The modern Beth is used in contemporary Hebrew.

Ancient Pictorial/Glyph: (a camel, a foot)
A camel is the ancient representation of Gimel,
symbolizing a carrier of loads and a bridge.

Introduction to Gimel

Embark on the third step of your Hebrew aleph-bet journey with Gimel. This letter, representing both motion and generosity, carries the spirit of journey and exchange. Just as a camel carries itself across vast deserts, Gimel carries forward the teachings of generosity and kindness.

Name and Spellings

Gimel occasionally spelled 'Gimmel' or 'Ghimel,' is a letter that signifies movement and the act of giving. As we explore Gimel, reflect on the fluidity and dynamism it brings to the Hebrew language.

Pronunciation Guide

It is pronounced 'gim-el' with a hard 'g' sound, as in 'girl and game.' The syllables break as 'gam' and 'el,' infusing the pronunciation with strength and clarity. This straightforward phonetic delivery embodies Gimel's robust nature.

Corresponding Greek and English Letters

Gimel corresponds to the Greek Gamma (Γ, γ) and the English letter G. As in its Greek and English counterparts, Gimel imparts a strong and clear sound, forming a vital component of the foundation of words.

Gimel represents the number 3.

This number signifies multiplicity and balance. It also symbolizes the flow of generosity, reflecting the dynamic nature of giving and receiving. Beth produces duality, and Gimel gathers these dual aspects into harmony and togetherness, emphasizing the stability inherent in the number three.

Meaning: Gimel as the Journeying Camel

The shape of Gimel is thought to resemble a vav with a yod as its foot, symbolizing a rich metaphor for travel and forward movement. This form embodies the ability to reach out and extend one's capacity for kindness and interaction with the world.

Historically, Gimel symbolized a camel, an animal essential for travel and trade in ancient cultures, particularly within desert environments. This pictorial origin conveys themes of endurance, movement, and carrying burdens over long distances. Gimel represents the essence of exploration and the kindness that accompanies a nomadic lifestyle—sharing resources and extending hospitality.

Gimel is traditionally associated with 'gemilut chasadim' (acts of kindness), reinforcing the letter's theme of generosity. It encourages carrying forward the values of kindness and benevolence, mirroring the camel's role in supporting and sustaining life through arduous journeys.

Interesting Fact

Gimel is unique in that it directly follows Beth in the Hebrew alphabet, and in mystical Israelite traditions, this sequence is symbolic. Beth represents the house, a place of starting and dwelling, while Gimel symbolizes the action of leaving or extending generosity beyond one's home, indicating a progression from stability to action.

Gimel's Connection to the Moon: In certain interpretations, Gimel is associated with the waxing and waning phases of the moon. These phases represent the cyclical nature of giving and receiving, emphasizing that periods of generosity are followed by times of restoration. As the moon waxes and wanes, so do acts of giving and replenishment. This cycle shows how charitable acts can lead to renewal and rebirth, affirming that sharing one's resources creates cosmic alignment that brings prosperity and blessings back to the giver.

The spelling of Gimel (Gimel, Mem, Lamed)

"Generosity (**Gimel**) flows through Wisdom (**Mem**) and
guides with Learning (**Lamed**)."

The Hebrew Spelling of Gimel

גמל

Gimel (ג): Represents generosity, symbolizing giving and the ability to nurture others.

Mem (מ): Signifies wisdom, emphasizing the flow of insight needed to give effectively and with intention.

Lamed (ל): Symbolizes learning, the guiding principle that helps channel generosity into meaningful actions.

Together, these letters show that Gimel embodies the journey of generosity, guided by wisdom and learning.

Chapter Engagement: Gimel Meditation

Meditating on Generosity

1. **Find a Quiet Space:** Sit comfortably in a calm, distraction-free place. Close your eyes and take a few deep breaths, inhaling through your nose and exhaling through your mouth.

2. **Visualize Gimel:** Imagine the letter Gimel in your mind, visualizing its form clearly. See the letter moving forward as if walking towards a destination, symbolizing generosity in action.

3. **Reflect on Generosity:** Contemplate how Gimel represents generosity and giving. Reflect on how acts of kindness and compassion propel individuals forward and uplift communities through selfless acts.

4. **Focus on Wisdom:** Reflect on the wisdom (Mem) and learning (Lamed) that guides generosity. Consider how giving from a place of understanding can bring transformative results and positively influence the lives of those around you.

5. **Set an Intention:** Take a deep breath and set an intention to practice generosity in a specific way. How can you embody the spirit of Gimel in your daily actions? What positive change can you create by giving thoughtfully and with purpose?

6. **Return to Presence:** Slowly open your eyes and return to the present. Carry this spirit of generosity forward, seeking opportunities to share your time, energy, and resources in meaningful ways.

CHAPTER 4

Daleth: The Humble Doorway

Daleth (ד)
Modern Hebrew Letter

Modern Daleth is used in contemporary Hebrew.

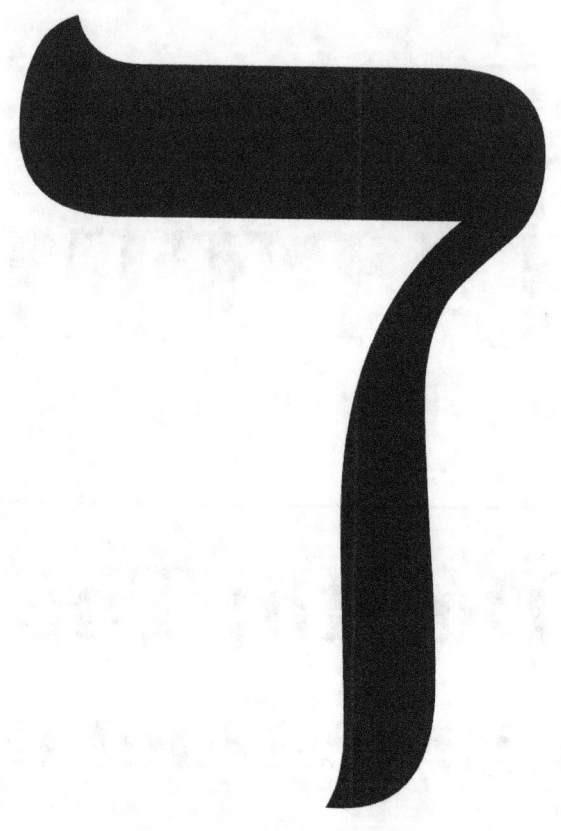

Ancient Pictorial/Glyph: (a door)

The door is the ancient representation of Daleth,
symbolizing a doorway or entryway.

Introduction to Daleth

Step through the fourth letter of the Hebrew aleph-beth: Daleth. This letter symbolizes a doorway, offering both an entrance into new experiences and a boundary that shelters and protects. Daleth invites you to explore the thresholds within life and spirit.

Name and Spellings

Daleth, also spelled 'Dalet,' is a letter that carries deep symbolic weight as the passage between different states of being. As we delve into Daleth, consider its role as both a separator and a connector within the Hebrew language.

Pronunciation Guide

Pronounced 'dah-let,' similar to the 'd' in 'door.' The simplicity of its pronunciation belies the depth of its meaning, representing both physical and metaphorical openings.

Corresponding Greek and English Letters

Daleth corresponds to the Greek Delta (Δ, δ) and the English letter D. Like its counterparts, Daleth constructs essential parts of language, often indicating division or derivation in words.

Numerical Value

Daleth represents the number 4.

This number symbolizes stability and structure, much like the four corners of a house or the four cardinal directions. It suggests solidity and the grounding of ideas into tangible realities, reflecting the foundational aspects that Daleth brings to life and language.

Daleth as the Humble Doorway

Daleth is fundamentally the door, the gate, which marks both the challenge of resistance and the state of selflessness and humility needed to pass through it. It serves as a gateway to deeper understanding, revealing the secrets of self-discovery and indicating how to traverse the gates to uncover one's own mystery of being. Daleth also shows how to return to the power of Aleph—the One source of all creation and being. Through Daleth, one progresses through Gimel and Beth, retracing steps back to the unity represented by Aleph.

From a cosmic viewpoint, Daleth is the symbolic boundary between the physical and spiritual realms. As the fourth letter of the Hebrew alphabet, Daleth aligns with the number four, which is often associated with the four elements (earth, air, fire, and water), the four directions (north, south, east, and west), and the four seasons. This alignment gives Daleth a universal and cosmic significance, suggesting that it acts as a portal through which divine wisdom flows into the material world.

Spiritually, Daleth embodies the concept of "dalut," which translates to humility or spiritual poverty. This humility is not about weakness but about recognizing that one's understanding is always limited compared to the vastness of cosmic knowledge. Daleth invites the individual to step through the doorway into the unknown with an open heart and mind, ready to receive divine truth and align with cosmic principles.

The ancient pictographic representation of Daleth resembles a door or a tent flap, emphasizing the concept of transition. In this cosmic sense, Daleth serves as a passage between the temporal and the eternal, the seen and the unseen. It acts as a reminder that the cosmos is a vast interconnected system and that every individual plays a role in this universal plan. This architectural shape reflects the concept of opening and closing, welcoming and guarding.

As a threshold, Daleth invites us to seek higher wisdom beyond the material limitations of our everyday world, urging us to align with cosmic cycles and divine will. By walking through the cosmic doorway of Daleth, we access a deeper understanding of our place in the universe and the importance of embracing humility as we journey toward spiritual enlightenment.

Interesting Fact

Daleth is seen as a symbol of humility and modesty. The word **"dal"** in Hebrew means **"poor"** or **"needy,"** and Daleth is believed to represent a doorway through which divine blessings can enter. Humility should not be mistaken for poverty. It is rather an attitude of receptiveness to higher wisdom. It is widely believed that Daleth remains accessible, providing an opportunity for spiritual enrichment and personal growth when you acknowledge your continuous need for learning and guidance.

Daleth is symbolically linked to the four directions: north, south, east, and west. This association emphasizes the idea of completeness and universality. In Kabbalistic thought, Daleth is the doorway through which divine influence flows to all corners of the world, reminding us that the divine presence encompasses every aspect of existence and is available to all who seek it.

The spelling of Daleth (Daleth, Lamed, Tav)

"The Door (**Daleth**) to True Authority (**Lamed**)

is Sealed with the Covenant (**Tav**)."

The Hebrew spelling of Daleth

דלת

Daleth (ד): Represents a door, symbolizing an entryway to new understanding and spiritual opportunity.

Lamed (ל): Symbolizes teaching and authority, representing the guidance and wisdom that helps one navigate the spiritual journey.

Tav (ת): Signifies the covenant, the sacred seal marking the fulfillment of the divine promise.

Together, these letters reveal that Daleth embodies the pathway to wisdom and spiritual fulfillment, secured through divine commitment.

Chapter Engagement: Daleth Meditation

Three-Minute Meditation for Daleth

Settle into Stillness: Sit in a comfortable position, close your eyes, and take a few slow, deep breaths. Inhale deeply through your nose and exhale gently through your mouth, calming your mind.

Visualize the Doorway: Imagine the letter Daleth as a doorway in your mind. Visualize its form clearly and see yourself standing before this doorway, ready to step through.

Contemplate Opportunity: Reflect on how Daleth represents a gateway to new understanding and spiritual opportunities. Consider how being open to learning and receiving guidance can unlock new doors in your life.

Focus on Authority: Think about the authority and wisdom represented by Lamed, which can guide you through Daleth. What knowledge or life lesson could help you navigate this doorway? How might you embody humility while also taking on new responsibilities?

Set Your Intention: As you take a few more deep breaths, set an intention to walk through the doorway. Think of one way you can embrace new learning, wisdom, or purpose in your daily life.

Return to Presence: Gradually open your eyes, feeling the calm of this meditative practice. Carry this feeling of stepping through the doorway into your day, using it as a reminder to remain open to new spiritual opportunities and growth.

CHAPTER 5

Heh: The Divine Breath

Heh (ה)
Modern Hebrew Letter
Modern Heh is used in contemporary Hebrew.

Ancient Pictorial/Glyph: (a window)

The window is the ancient representation of Heh,
symbolizing an opening or breath.

Introduction to Heh

Explore the fifth letter of the Hebrew aleph-beth: Heh. This letter embodies the essence of divine breath and revelation. As a symbol deeply ingrained in spiritual contexts, Heh opens windows to new insights and divine inspirations.

Name and Spellings

Heh, also known simply as 'H' and sometimes 'He,' is a letter that evokes the act of expression and the subtle force of the breath. As we explore Heh, consider its role in articulating and revealing the hidden.

Pronunciation Guide

Heh is pronounced like 'hay' with a light, breathy 'h' sound similar to the 'h' in 'hope.' This soft exhalation reflects its intrinsic meaning as the breath of life and spirit.

Corresponding Greek and English Letters

Heh corresponds to the Greek Eta (H, η) and the English letter H. Just like its counterparts, Heh is often a silent harbinger of a deeper presence in words, subtly influencing their meanings without overtly asserting itself.

Numerical Value

Heh represents the number 5.

This number is often associated with grace, mercy, and protection. It underscores the concept of divine grace permeating through the cosmos, offering a protective, life-giving force that Heh metaphorically breathes into the world.

Heh, as the Divine Breath and Window

Heh symbolizes a multitude of profound concepts: the divine breath, a window, revelation, 'behold,' and light. It is often visualized as resembling a person with arms raised a posture evoking revelation and receptivity. This form symbolizes openness and the channeling of energy from higher realms into the material world. The shape of Heh consists of two components: 2 vertical and a horizontal line that forms an open structure on one side. This architectural openness is emblematic of a window, providing a view and a passageway to understanding and deeper insight.

Heh is often seen as the symbol of transformation and the creative power of divine speech. When placed at the end of a Hebrew verb, it changes the meaning to signify transformation or causation, highlighting its ability to turn potential into reality. This transformative quality also reflects the concept of teshuvah (repentance), which involves a shift in consciousness toward alignment with the divine will. This letter illustrates the process of growth and change through receptivity, where openness allows one to receive divine wisdom and bring positive transformation into the world.

Heh is believed to connect heaven and earth. Its open window-like structure is a passageway through which divine inspiration flows into the material realm. Heh's presence in the divine name of Yahweh emphasizes its role in revealing spiritual truths that transcend the mundane. It represents the breath that sustains all life, reminding humanity of its divine origin. Heh encourages individuals to cultivate openness, reflect on higher principles, and channel spiritual insight into their daily thoughts and actions.

Heh's dual nature as both an expression of the divine breath and a vessel for divine light and wisdom highlights its role in the flow of spiritual energy into human experience. Heh's presence in the Divine name Yahweh embeds an element of the divine in key scriptural concepts, adding a dimension of inhalation, exhalation, and life force that reinforces the notion of creation and the existential breath that permeates through speech and thought.

Interesting Fact

The addition of Heh to the Biblical Abram's name caused him to become Abraham and Sarai to Sarah. The Hebrew Bible signifies their transformation and readiness to fulfill their divine missions. This letter thus represents divine intervention and the elevation of human life through spiritual grace.

Heh is believed to symbolize the five senses, representing the ways in which humanity interacts with and understands the world. This connection to the five senses highlights Heh's role in translating divine inspiration into a tangible human experience. By aligning one's senses with spiritual insight, Heh serves as a reminder that everyday perception can lead to deeper understanding when focused through the lens of higher awareness. This perspective emphasizes the balance between the spiritual and the physical, guiding individuals to infuse their daily actions with wisdom and purpose.

Spelling of Heh (Heh, Heh)

"The **Window (Heh)** reveals **Understanding (Heh).**"

The Hebrew spelling of Heh

הה

Heh (ה): Represents a window, offering a passageway to divine revelation and insight.

Heh (ה): It also symbolizes understanding, emphasizing the openness to receive spiritual wisdom and the willingness to express it.

In this combination, Heh embodies the connection between revelation and understanding, providing a window through which divine inspiration flows.

Chapter Engagement: Meditation for Heh

Meditating on Openness and Revelation

Settle and Focus: Find a quiet, comfortable space to sit. Close your eyes, take a deep breath through your nose, and exhale through your mouth. Let your body relax and settle into stillness.

Visualize Heh: Picture the letter Heh in your mind as a window, symbolizing openness and the passage to higher wisdom. Visualize light streaming through the window, illuminating the space around you and revealing new possibilities.

Reflect on Revelation: Consider how Heh represents revelation and how openness can lead to greater understanding. What new insights or opportunities are available to you if you open yourself up to receive them?

Channel Spiritual Energy: With each breath, imagine the divine breath filling your mind and heart, channeling spiritual energy into your being. Let the light of Heh guide you towards clarity and understanding.

Set an Intention: Take a deep breath and think of one way you can embody the openness of Heh. How can you allow new wisdom to illuminate your actions and bring positive change to your life?

Return to Presence: Slowly open your eyes and feel yourself fully grounded in the present moment. Carry this renewed sense of openness and spiritual energy with you throughout your day.

CHAPTER 6

Wav: The Connecting Hook

Wav (ו)
Modern Hebrew Letter

Modern Wav is used in contemporary Hebrew.

Ancient Pictorial/Glyph: (a hook)

A hook or nail is the ancient representation of Wav,
symbolizing that which joins.

Introduction to Wav

Explore the 6th letter of the Hebrew aleph-beth: Wav. This letter is a fundamental connector within the Hebrew text, linking words, clauses, and concepts, illustrating the interconnectedness of all things.

Name and Spellings

Wav, also spelled as **'Vav'** or **'Waw,'** is a letter that embodies connection and continuity. As you delve deeper into Wav, appreciate its pivotal role in bridging elements within the Hebrew language and narrative structures.

Pronunciation Guide

Pronounced **'vahv'** or **'wahv,'** depending on dialectical variations, it has a soft **'v'** or a gentle **'w'** sound, similar to the **'v'** in **'victory'** or the **'w'** in **'water.'** This versatile sound reflects its linguistic flexibility and adaptability.

Corresponding Greek and English Letters

Wav corresponds to the Greek Upsilon **(Y, υ)** and the English letters **V** or **W**. Like its counterparts, **Wav** is versatile in its usage, often altering its role from a consonant to a vowel marker in various contexts.

Numerical Value

Wav represents the number 6. This number symbolizes the six days of the creation of the world, as well as the six physical dimensions: right, left, front, back, up, and down. It reflects the foundational structure of the physical universe, underscoring Wav's role in providing balance and stability.

Meaning: Wav is the Connecting Hook

Wav is often referred to by names such as **'hook,'** **'spear,'** or **'tent peg,'** each emphasizing its function as a connector or anchor. The letter represents the ladder of Jacob (Yaakov) rooted in the earth with its head in the heavens, symbolizing the aspiration to connect the mundane with the divine.

Wav's form is straightforward yet profound, a single vertical line that resembles a hook. This simple shape is emblematic of its primary function in Hebrew: to connect. Linguistically, Wav is used as a conjunction to connect sentences or clauses, often translated as **'and.'**

Beyond its grammatical uses, Wav has deep spiritual implications. It is a channel between the divine and the earthly, mirroring the conceptual link it provides in the text. Wav represents the vertical line connecting spiritual and material realms, facilitating the flow of divine energy to the earth and symbolizing the continuous interaction between these dimensions.

Wav's presence in the Tetragrammaton, the four-letter name YHWH, underscores its integral role in divine expression. It is the connecting element in the sacred name, emphasizing unity and continuity in the divine essence. Wav represents the male, the fertilizing agent that brings life, abundance, continuity, and addition.

Interesting Fact

In biblical symbolism, Wav is considered the connecting force in the cosmos. It is traditionally viewed as the 'and' that binds the words of creation, mirroring its role in Genesis, where Yahweh connects the sky and the water, as well as the earth and the heavens. This role is metaphysically extended to the belief that Wav acts as a bridge or conduit between the spiritual and material worlds, embodying the divine continuity throughout creation.

Wav is viewed as a pivotal element in maintaining cosmic balance and facilitating the seamless flow of divine energies, solidifying its role as a foundational aspect of spiritual structure.

Wav is the **'hook'** that connects the divine to the earthly, often associated with the ladder of Jacob's dream. It is believed to represent the axis mundi, or the world axis, which serves as a spiritual bridge between heaven and earth. This concept is reinforced by the shape of Wav, which resembles a vertical line, symbolizing the flow of divine energy downwards into the material world while simultaneously drawing human consciousness upwards toward the spiritual.

Wav's numerical value of 6 is also considered the number of creations, as the world was created in six days. Therefore, it represents the harmonious integration of the divine within the cosmos.

Spelling of Wav (Wav, Wav)

"The Hook (Wav) connects with Guidance (Wav)."

The Hebrew spelling of Wav

וו

Wav (ו): Symbolizes a hook, representing the link that connects the divine and earthly realms.

Wav (ו): Also symbolizes guidance, highlighting the importance of connection and alignment.

In this combination, Wav embodies the concept of creating a bridge between different realms and facilitating spiritual alignment.

Chapter Engagement

Meditating on Connection and Alignment

Find Stillness: Sit comfortably, close your eyes, and take a few slow, deep breaths. Inhale deeply through your nose and exhale through your mouth, letting your body relax and your mind calm.

Visualize Wav: Picture the letter Wav in your mind, seeing it as a vertical line that connects heaven and earth. Imagine it as a channel through which divine energy flows down to the material world while also drawing your spirit upward.

Reflect on Connection: Contemplate how Wav symbolizes connection, acting as a bridge between the divine and the earthly. Think about the different ways that spiritual energy flows through you and how it connects to your thoughts, emotions, and actions.

Align with Purpose: With each breath, visualize energy flowing through Wav, aligning your intentions and actions with your higher purpose. Let this energy guide you in finding harmony between your physical and spiritual aspects.

Set an Intention: Take a few deep breaths and set an intention to embody the connection and alignment of Wav. How can you better connect with divine wisdom while grounding yourself in daily life?

Return to Presence: Slowly open your eyes and return to the present moment. Feel centered and aligned, ready to carry this sense of purpose and spiritual connection into your day.

CHAPTER 7

Zayin: The Sword of Spirit

Zayin (ז)
Modern Hebrew Letter

Modern Zayin is used in contemporary Hebrew.

Ancient Pictorial/Glyph: (a sword, plowing tool)

A sword is the ancient representation of Zayin, symbolizing a weapon or any implementation of war. It is also represented as a plowing tool.

Introduction to Zayin

Venture deeper into the Hebrew aleph-beth with Zayin, the seventh letter. Zayin is a symbol of both warfare and nourishment, encapsulating the dual nature of protection and destruction. This letter invites you to explore the themes of conflict and resolution, highlighting the spiritual battles and the strength derived from them.

Name and Spellings

Zayin sometimes spelled 'Zayn,' resonates with themes of battle and spirit. As we examine Zayin, reflect on its sharpness and what it protects or fights for within the spiritual realm of the Hebrew texts.

Pronunciation Guide

Pronounced 'zah-yin,' similar to the 'z' in 'zebra.' Zayin's sharp, clear sound mirrors its symbolic representation as a sword, cutting through ambiguity to reveal deeper truths.

Corresponding Greek and English Letters

Zayin corresponds to the Greek Zeta (Z, ζ) and the English letter Z. Like these counterparts, Zayin is relatively rare but significant, marking important moments and terms in Hebrew literature.

Numerical Value

Zayin represents the number 7. This number is spiritually significant across many cultures and is often associated with completeness and divine perfection. It symbolizes the completion of a cycle, such as the seven days of creation, reflecting Zayin's role in marking spiritual completeness and rest.

Zayin as the Sword of Spirit

Zayin's complex symbolism as a sword, nourisher, and crown invites deep reflection on the ways we wield power and influence in our own lives. It embodies the paradox of a weapon and a nourisher. Zayin, as a 'sword' or 'weapon,' carries a multifaceted symbolism that spans defense, nourishment, and royalty. Zayin, shaped like a sword, symbolizes a spectrum of profound concepts—spirit, sustenance, and struggle.

As a sword, it emphasizes its role as a tool of defense and an instrument in both physical and spiritual battles. This imagery emphasizes Zayin's representation in scriptural interpretation, where it signifies the struggle against wrongdoing and the enforcement of justice. As a sword, Zayin stands for movement and the inherent struggles of existence. It symbolizes the eternal battles between opposites, the celestial wrestling of Jacob, representing the struggle for spiritual and physical sustenance.

Zayin captures the dual nature of conflict and provision, serving both as a weapon in battle and as a tool that nourishes. The aspect of 'nourishment' associated with Zayin is less about physical sustenance and more about the sustenance of the spirit and moral fortitude. Zayin nourishes the soul by upholding truth and righteousness, providing 'food' for spiritual and ethical growth. Zayin embodies the belief that true strength is found in both the ability to conquer and the promotion and upholding of justice and morality.

Zayin serves as a reminder of the ongoing connection between the spiritual and material worlds, where every action and thought reflects divine intervention. It challenges us to embrace our roles as conduits of divine will, balancing the material aspects of our lives with spiritual truths and striving for harmony that enriches both realms. It asks us to consider how we might use our abilities not just to defend what we believe in but also to enrich and elevate the moral and spiritual well-being of the earth.

Zayin is also the driving force within us that compels speech, action, and the pursuit of life. It embodies the dynamic interplay between receiving divine influences and the human responsibility to act upon them, urging us to initiate, live, and transcend our limitations.

It represents the 7th day of Shabbat (Sabbath), a sacred time of rest and spirituality that completes the cycle of the six days of creation. The Sabbath embodies the spiritual dimension that activates and sustains the physical world, marking Zayin as a source of all movement and life-giving energy.

Interesting Fact

In the rich tapestry of mysticism and scripture, the number seven holds profound significance, embodied in the letter Zayin. This connection is most prominently observed in the observance of the Sabbath, the seventh day dedicated to rest and spiritual reflection, which completes the cycle of the six days of creation. The Sabbath is not merely a day of physical rest but also a spiritual experience that reaffirms the divine covenant, providing deeper nourishment that the soul yearns for throughout the temporal labors of the week.

Beyond the Sabbath, the number seven manifests in the concept of the 'seven oaths' and the 'seven seals,' each representing layers of commitment and revelation within spiritual practice. The seven oaths, as discussed in mystical texts, bind the physical creation with the spiritual realms, ensuring that the actions in the material world resonate with higher divine purposes. These oaths serve as spiritual statutes that govern the interactions between the divine and the earthly, symbolizing the sacred responsibilities entrusted to humanity.

Similarly, the seven seals, often referenced in eschatological contexts, represent stages of unfolding divine revelation and judgment. Each seal, when metaphorically 'broken,' reveals deeper insights into divine will and the ultimate reconciliation of all creation with its Creator. Zayin, embodying this number, thus serves as a key to unlocking these deeper dimensions of spiritual truth and cosmic order.

The recurring theme of the number seven in these contexts underscores the cyclic and complete nature of divine interaction with the world, mediated through Zayin. It highlights the belief that spiritual progression involves phases of growth, challenge, and renewal, each marked by divine grace and wisdom.

Spelling of Zayin

(Zayin, Yod, Nun)

"The Sword (Zayin) draws upon Divine Energy (Yod) to bring forth Life (Nun)."

The Hebrew spelling of Zayin is

זין

Zayin (ז): Represents a sword, symbolizing the cutting edge of justice and spiritual striving.

Yod (י): Signifies divine energy, the essential spark of life and wisdom.

Nun (ן): Symbolizes life and movement, representing the eternal cycle of growth and renewal.

Together, these letters embody the concept of spiritual striving that draws upon divine energy to manifest life and movement.

Chapter Engagement: Zayin Meditation

Meditating on Striving and Justice

1. **Find Calm:** Sit comfortably, close your eyes, and take several deep breaths, inhaling through your nose and exhaling through your mouth. Allow your mind and body to relax.

2. **Visualize Zayin:** Picture the letter Zayin in your mind, visualizing it as a sword. Imagine its form clearly, shining with light and pointing upwards, symbolizing spiritual striving and the pursuit of justice.

3. **Reflect on Justice:** Contemplate how Zayin represents the desire to strive for balance, integrity, and righteousness. Consider how the sword of Zayin cuts through illusions to reveal truth and protect what is just.

4. **Channel Divine Energy:** With each breath, visualize the sword drawing in divine energy from Yod, infusing your spirit with strength and purpose. Allow this energy to guide your thoughts, aligning them with the pursuit of justice.

5. **Set an Intention:** Take a few deep breaths and set an intention to embody the spirit of Zayin. How can you strive for justice in your daily actions and cut through distractions to align with your higher values?

6. **Return to Presence:** Gradually open your eyes, grounded and centered. Carry this determination and energy forward into your day, striving for balance and justice in all your actions.

CHAPTER 8

Chet: The Life Gateway

Chet (ח)
Modern Hebrew Letter
Modern Chet is used in contemporary Hebrew.

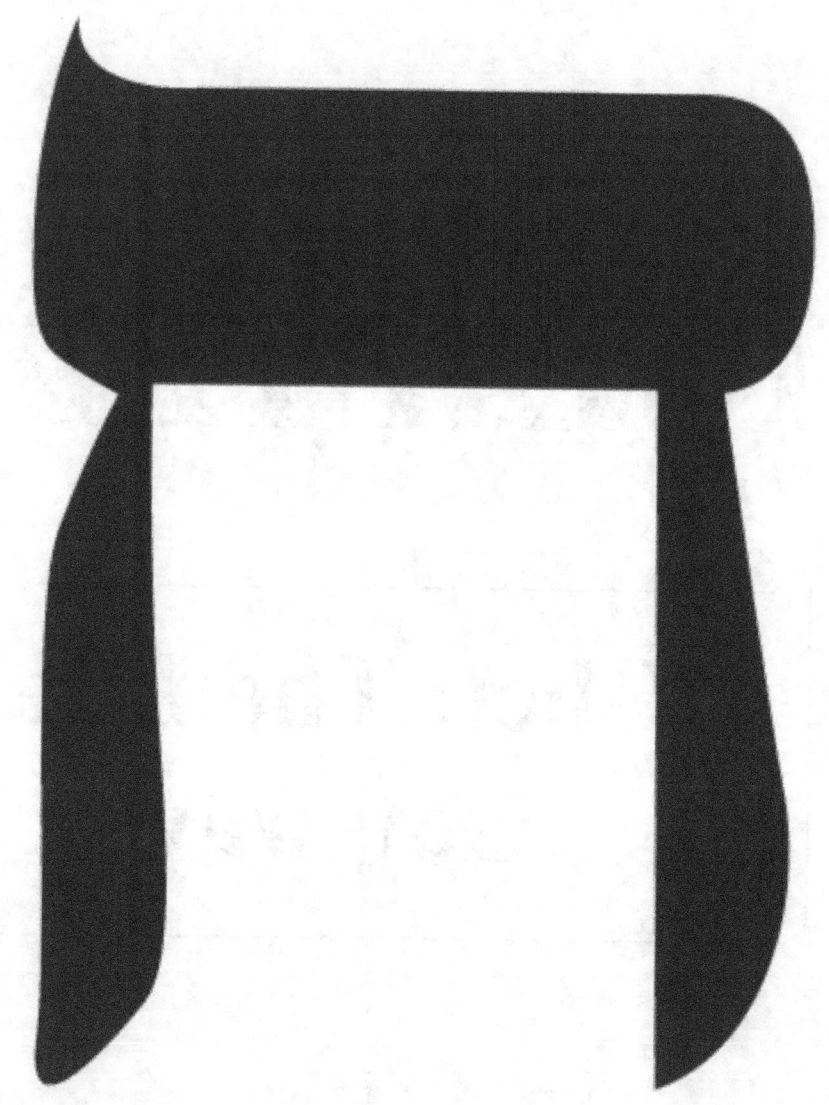

Ancient Pictorial/Glyph: (a fence or wall)
The ancient representation of Chet symbolizes a fence or enclosure.

Introduction to Chet

Progress to the eighth letter of the Hebrew aleph-beth: Chet. This letter symbolizes an enclosure but also a new beginning, representing the dichotomy between boundary and birth. It invites exploration of spaces both protected and sacred, encapsulating themes of life and sanctity.

Name and Spellings

Chet, sometimes also spelled as **'Het, Cheth, or Heth,'** is a key to understanding boundaries and sacred spaces within the Hebrew language. As we delve into Chet, ponder its role in forming words that encapsulate concepts of life, protection, and sanctity.

Pronunciation Guide

Pronounced **'chet'** with a throaty, breathy sound, much like the **'ch'** in the Scottish **'loch'** or the German **'Bach.'** This deep, resonant pronunciation echoes the letter's significance in symbolizing barriers that are both protective and defining.

Corresponding Greek and English Letters

Chet does not have a direct counterpart in Greek or English alphabets, highlighting its unique role in Hebrew. Its sound and symbolism are distinct within the context of the Hebrew language, emphasizing its special character. The letters 'ch' or 'h' are often used in English when writing words using chet.

Numerical Value

Chet represents the number 8. This number is often associated with transcendence, infinity, and higher realms of spiritual existence. It signifies abundance and the cyclic nature of life, mirroring the biblical concept of circumcision on the eighth day.

Chet as the Life Gateway

Chet's shape resembles a fence or wall, suggesting its function as a boundary and protector. These boundaries are not merely restrictive; they create a defined, sacred space essential for life and spiritual growth. This protective aspect makes Chet a symbol of both separation and enclosure, providing safety and sanctity.

Expanding its symbolism, Chet visually resembles a fence or tent wall, suggesting its role as a boundary and protector. It also represents Chet defining and separating sacred spaces within a nomadic context. This separation is fundamental, as it helps maintain purity and sanctity by delineating what is inside (sacred) from what is outside (profane).

However, these boundaries are not merely restrictive; they create a defined, safe, and consecrated space. This aspect of Chet emphasizes its function in creating and protecting sacred spaces, such as those used for worship and spiritual retreats.

Spiritually, Chet is often associated with the 'Chai' (חי), which means 'life' in Hebrew. This connection highlights the life-affirming qualities of Chet, where the boundaries it creates are essential for fostering life and spiritual growth. It symbolizes the entrance to a new phase of existence, akin to passing through a gateway that leads to deeper understanding and spiritual awakening.

Chet is also considered as representing the union of heaven and earth, bridging the spiritual and the physical. It is a gateway through which divine energies flow into the material world, facilitating spiritual insight and enlightenment. This mystical aspect of Chet stresses its significance as both a physical boundary and a spiritual passage.

The letter Chet, therefore, embodies a profound dichotomy: it serves as both a protective boundary and a gateway to new beginnings, reflecting the dual nature of sanctity and life that it represents.

Chet is a gateway to new beginnings, akin to passing through a door that leads to a deeper spiritual awakening. It embodies the journey from the finite to the infinite, making visible the invisible spiritual truths that govern existence.

Interesting Fact

Chet was a symbol of life and transcendence in ancient teachings. It was closely associated with the concept of new beginnings and renewal. For instance, circumcision was performed on the eighth day after a male child's birth, marking a covenantal relationship between the child and the divine. This practice emphasized the idea of transcending the natural order to form a deeper connection with Yahweh, embodying the spiritual aspirations that Chet symbolizes. The letter also represents a protective enclosure, reminding the Israelites of the importance of maintaining spiritual integrity and communal unity.

Chet is a symbol of the binding force that connects the upper and lower worlds. Chet is often linked with the concept of divine protection, representing the hidden sanctuary within oneself that houses spiritual potential. This sanctuary is the point where the divine spark rests and where spiritual energies gather, symbolizing a doorway to deeper esoteric knowledge. In this way, Chet is the hidden passage to unlocking inner wisdom and accessing spiritual mysteries that transcend the material world.

Spelling of Chet

(Chet, Yod, Tav)

"The Life Gate (Chet) is Enlightened by Divine Spark (Yod) and
Sealed by Covenant (Tav)."

The Hebrew spelling of Chet

ח י ת

Chet (ח): Symbolizes a gate or fence, representing protection, life, and a gateway to spiritual understanding.

Yod (י): Represents a divine spark, the spiritual energy that illuminates the path forward.

Tav (ת): Signifies the covenant, sealing the journey with the promise of divine protection and fulfillment.

Together, these letters reflect Chet's role as a gateway to spiritual enlightenment, guided by divine wisdom and sealed by divine commitment.

Chapter Engagement: Chet Meditation

Meditating on Life and Spiritual Growth

Prepare and Center: Sit comfortably, close your eyes, and take a few deep breaths, inhaling through your nose and exhaling through your mouth. Allow yourself to become centered and relaxed.

Visualize Chet: Imagine the letter Chet in your mind, visualizing it as a gate or ladder. Picture light shining through this gate, symbolizing the life force and spiritual growth that Chet represents.

Reflect on Protection: Consider how Chet represents both a protective enclosure and a gateway to higher spiritual understanding. Think about the areas of your life where protection is needed and how being open to spiritual insights can help you find solutions.

Channel Divine Energy: As you breathe deeply, visualize divine energy flowing through Chet, illuminating your spirit and revealing hidden wisdom. Let this energy fill you with vitality and clarity.

Set an Intention: Take a deep breath and set an intention to align with the symbolism of Chet. How can you protect your own inner life while remaining open to new spiritual possibilities?

Return to Presence: Gradually open your eyes, carrying a renewed sense of life and purpose. Move forward with the openness to spiritual growth and wisdom that Chet represents.

CHAPTER 9

Teth: The Hidden Goodness

Teth (ט)
Modern Hebrew Letter

Modern Teth is used in contemporary Hebrew.

Ancient Pictorial/Glyph: (a basket)

The ancient representation of Teth is a basket.

Introduction to Teth

Continue your exploration of the Hebrew aleph-beth with Teth, the ninth letter. Often associated with hidden goodness and inward qualities, Teth invites introspection and reflection on the deeper, often concealed aspects of life and spirituality.

Name and Spellings

Teth, occasionally also spelled **'Tet,'** is a letter that encompasses profound spiritual mysteries. As we explore Teth, consider its enigmatic nature and the themes of concealment and revelation it embodies.

Pronunciation Guide

Pronounced **'tet,'** similar to the **'t'** in **'tether.'** This sound is firm and grounding, reflecting Teth's associations with earthiness and substantiality in the physical world.

Corresponding Greek and English Letters

Teth does not have a direct counterpart in Greek or English alphabets, which highlights its unique place in Hebrew. Its distinctiveness emphasizes the special spiritual and symbolic meanings Teth holds within the Hebrew language.

Numerical Value

Teth represents the number 9. This number often symbolizes completeness, truth, and the attainment of a spiritual journey. It invites a look at the cyclical nature of life and the layers of wisdom that can be uncovered through deep, reflective thought.

Teth as the Hidden Goodness

Teth's form resembles a container or a basket, which implies its role in holding and containing. Metaphorically, this shape embodies the concealed elements of life encapsulated by Teth, such as spiritual treasures and truths that can only be revealed through introspection and comprehension.

The symbolism of Teth extends to embody the concept of 'hidden goodness,' like a seed buried in the earth that holds the potential for life and growth. This hidden aspect is essential in many spiritual traditions, where the most profound truths are discovered beneath the surface of the mundane.

Tet symbolizes the goodness inherent in all creation. Teth represents the concealed good that exists within everything. It is connected with concepts of purity and impurity, guiding us to choose the good while understanding that even within difficult circumstances, hidden goodness can be found.

Tet challenges us to look beyond appearances to find the intrinsic good hidden within every situation, every challenge, and even within every person. It is often hidden and requires human effort to uncover and reveal its presence. This search for hidden goodness is not merely an exercise in optimism but a profound journey into the depths of faith and understanding, where the complexities of life often veil the true nature of things.

Tet embodies the kindness and mercy of creation, teaching us to discern between good and bad. By choosing the good, we cleanse and purify, erasing previous misdeeds. Tet encapsulates the idea that nothing is truly lost or wasted and that all things are eternal. It encompasses the infinite while giving rise to the finite.

Tet also represents the natural way (teva) and the way of goodness (tov), constantly searching for truth. It reflects an ongoing journey, a quest for knowledge, and a struggle to uncover deeper truths.

Tet symbolizes femininity and pregnancy. It represents the kindness and mercy of creation and the principle that everything is eternal. The letter's feminine essence is clear in its connection to the number 9, symbolizing both completion and the nine months of pregnancy. Its shape resembles a womb or spiral, a vessel where transformation and change occur. Tet is the essence of the feminine, containing and nurturing everything within.

Interesting Fact

Tet is the only Hebrew letter that has a symmetrical shape, facing both forward and backward. This symmetry reflects the balanced and cyclical nature of the universe, emphasizing the importance of maintaining harmony in one's journey. The symmetry also symbolizes the idea of reflection and introspection, encouraging individuals to look inward and recognize that every action has both visible and hidden consequences. This unique quality of Tet invites us to balance our thoughts and deeds, always striving to bring our intentions and actions into alignment.

Tet's numeric value of 9 is believed to be connected to the concept of hidden potential and spiritual enlightenment. Number 9 is associated with special prayers of gratitude for the hidden miracles that sustain life daily. This association emphasizes Tet's role in uncovering the deeper layers of reality and appreciating the subtle blessings that often go unnoticed but are essential to growth and fulfillment.

Spelling of Teth

(Teth, Yod, Tav)

"The Wheel (Teth) carries the Divine Spark (Yod)
towards Truth (Tav)."

The Hebrew spelling of Teth

ת י ט

Teth (ט): Symbolizes a wheel or container, representing transformation, potential, and the cycle of life.

Yod (י): Represents the divine spark, the energy that animates life and drives positive change.

Tav (ת): Signifies truth and fulfillment, sealing the journey with a promise of completeness.

Together, these letters reflect Teth's role as a wheel of transformation, guiding the divine spark toward ultimate fulfillment.

Chapter Engagement: Teth Meditation

Meditating on Potential and Transformation

1. **Find Stillness:** Sit comfortably, close your eyes, and take a few deep breaths. Inhale deeply through your nose and exhale through your mouth, letting yourself relax.

2. **Visualize Teth:** Imagine the letter Teth in your mind as a wheel or container. See it filled with light, representing transformation and potential. Visualize this wheel spinning slowly, embodying the cycle of life.

3. **Reflect on Potential:** Consider the concept of potential and how Teth represents the hidden good within all things. Think of one area in your life where there is unrealized potential and consider how you can nurture it into positive change.

4. **Channel the Divine Spark:** With each breath, visualize a divine spark (Yod) inside the wheel of Teth, infusing your spirit with energy and inspiration. Let this spark guide you toward truth and fulfillment.

5. **Set an Intention:** Take a deep breath and set an intention to align with Teth's transformative energy. How can you use the wheel of Teth to channel your inner potential and drive positive change?

6. **Return to Presence:** Gradually open your eyes, grounded and energized. Carry this sense of potential and purpose with you as you navigate the day, always looking for the hidden good in your experiences.

CHAPTER 10

Yod: The Divine Spark

Yod (')
Modern Hebrew Letter

Modern Yod is used in contemporary Hebrew.

Ancient Pictorial/Glyph: (a hand, fist, and arm)

A hand, a fist, or a forearm symbolize the ancient representation of Yod.

Introduction to Yod

Advance to the tenth letter of the Hebrew aleph-beth: **Yod**. The smallest letter in the Hebrew alphabet, **Yod,** holds immense significance and is often considered the atom of consciousness in Kabbalistic thought. It represents the initial point of existence, from which all creation expands.

Name and Spellings

Yod, also spelled **'Yud,'** is a foundational letter in Hebrew. It reflects beginnings and the minute yet powerful essence of the divine. As we explore Yod, we should reflect on its role as a source and a spark in both language and the cosmos.

Pronunciation Guide

Pronounced **'yode,'** similar to the **'y'** in **'year.'** This brief, sharp sound captures the quick ignition of all things, reflecting Yod's representation as a spark or seed from which greater concepts and realities bloom.

Corresponding Greek and English Letters

Yod corresponds to the Greek Iota **(I, ι)** and the English letter **I** or **Y.** Like its counterparts, Yod is small but fundamental, often involved in crafting essential elements of language and meaning.

Numerical Value

Yod represents the number 10. This number is symbolic of perfection, law, and responsibility. It is the base of the decimal system, mirroring Yod's role as a point of origin in metaphysical and practical realms.

Yod, the Divine Spark

Yod is a symbol of the Holy One, the Creator. It is the foundation of all foundations. Yod represents a mere dot, a divine point of energy, the hidden Divine spark that causes everything to be. Yod is the hand, a closed hand, or a fist. It represents a pivotal drop in the concentrated power of Yahweh. It represents the power of the spirit to govern and guide the matter.

It is Unity within multiplicity, one whole made of many parts. Yod is used to form all the other letters, and since Yahweh uses the letters as the building blocks of creation, Yod shows Yahweh's omnipresence. In fact, the word יוד (yod) itself depicts something of the geometry of creation.

Yod's form is minimalistic, appearing as just a dot or a small stroke, yet it is considered the starting point of the divine name and creation in many mystical texts. This tiny letter is often seen as encapsulating the entire universe, symbolizing the omnipresent yet compact force of the divine.

Spiritually, Yod represents the divine spark within each aspect of creation, the seed from which complexities grow. It is like a hand that initiates action, movement, and creation, guiding the materialization of thoughts and spirits into tangible realities. Yod is the starting letter of God Yahweh's name, underscoring its quintessential role in forming the universe and in divine speech.

The letter Yod challenges us to recognize the potential in the smallest of beginnings, encouraging mindfulness of how minute actions or thoughts can have expansive and profound effects. It teaches us about the essence of purity and the concentrated power of creation that can be directed for transformative purposes.

Interesting Fact

Yod is considered the fundamental 'spark' of the spirit in all living beings. Its stature as the smallest letter underscores the teaching that great things often begin in humble forms, and that true power and essence are not always visible or ostentatious.

Yod is the smallest letter in the Hebrew aleph-beth, yet it plays a crucial role in shaping every other letter. Every Hebrew letter contains an element of Yod in its design, symbolizing the concept that all creation begins with a single divine point. Yod represents the initial spark of creation and consciousness, emphasizing that the greatest achievements start from small beginnings. The numeric value of Yod is 10, which is a sacred number representing both divine order and human potential.

Spelling of Yod

(Yod, Wav, Daleth)

"The Divine Spark (Yod) connects (Wav) through
the Doorway (Daleth)."

The Hebrew spelling of Yod

י ו ד

Yod (י): Represents the divine spark, the point of creation that ignites life and consciousness.

Wav (ו): Symbolizes connection, bridging the divine and the material realms.

Daleth (ד): Signifies a doorway, marking the passageway to new understanding and potential.

Together, these letters embody Yod's role as the divine spark that connects through a doorway, opening up new paths of awareness and understanding.

Chapter Engagement: Yod Meditation

Meditating on Divine Potential

Find Calm: Sit comfortably, close your eyes, and breathe deeply, inhaling through your nose and exhaling through your mouth. Let your body relax into stillness.

Visualize Yod: Picture the letter Yod in your mind as a small spark of light. Visualize this spark floating in the darkness, glowing with energy and potential. See it clearly, illuminating everything around it.

Reflect on Creation: Contemplate how Yod represents the divine spark and the potential for creation. Think about an area in your life where this potential lies, waiting to be realized. What small step can you take to kindle this spark into something greater?

Channel Connection: As you breathe deeply, imagine this spark expanding through Wav, creating a bridge to a new doorway (Daleth). Let this connection guide you through this doorway and into new possibilities for growth and fulfillment.

Set an Intention: Take a deep breath and set an intention to recognize the small divine sparks in your life. How can you nurture these sparks and connect them to new opportunities?

Return to Presence: Gradually open your eyes and feel yourself grounded in the present moment. Carry this renewed sense of divine potential with you throughout the day, noticing the sparks of possibility all around you.

CHAPTER 11

Kaph: The Palm
of Potential

Kaph (ך,כ)
Modern Hebrew Letter

Modern Kaph and its final or sofit form are used in contemporary Hebrew.

Ancient Pictorial/Glyph: (a palm or a hand)

The ancient representation of Kaph symbolizes a vessel or receiving.

Introduction to Kaph

Dive into the eleventh letter of the Hebrew aleph-beth: Kaph. This letter, resembling a cupped hand, symbolizes receiving and holding, reflecting the capacity to contain and channel blessings, knowledge, and potential.

Name and Spellings

Kaph, also spelled 'Kaf,' represents the literal meaning of 'palm' in Hebrew. As we delve deeper into Kaph, consider its embracing and encompassing nature, reflecting on how it holds and shapes the energies and gifts life offers.

Pronunciation Guide

Pronounced **'Kaph,'** similar to the **'k'** in **'kite.'** The sound is crisp and controlled, mirroring the form and function of a hand that grasps or shapes material reality.

Corresponding Greek and English Letters

Kaph corresponds to the Greek Kappa (K, κ) and the English letter K. These counterparts share a similar sound, playing fundamental roles in the formation of words and concepts within their respective languages.

Numerical Value

Kaph represents the number 20. This number often symbolizes completion and sufficiency, reflecting Kaph's capacity to hold and encompass a full cycle of experience or wisdom.

Kaph as the Palm of Potential

Kaph's form visually mimics a cupped hand or a vessel, illustrating its primary function to hold, shape, and channel. This symbolic hand grasps physical objects and captures intangible qualities such as blessings, skills, and possibilities. It emphasizes the potential to both receive from and give back to the world, highlighting the dual nature of interaction and exchange.

Kaph is a container of divine energy. It is like the palm of Yahweh's hand that both gives and measures out the essence of life and spirit. This letter invites introspection on how we manage and distribute the resources, gifts, and energies we possess. It asks us to consider how we can use our own 'palms'—our abilities and capacities—to make a meaningful impact.

Kaph's presence in words related to bending or curving, like **'Kaphuf' (bent),** underscores the concept of humility and receptiveness. It represents the bending down to receive wisdom and then rising to act upon it, embodying the cycle of learning and application that leads to spiritual and intellectual growth.

Kaph resembles an open hand and carries deep symbolism connected to giving, receiving, and the power of choice. In Hebrew, Kaph is the palm, reflecting the hand's ability to shape, create, and offer support. The letter's open-hand form symbolizes the readiness to receive divine blessing and the willingness to bestow kindness. This dynamic interplay between giving and receiving teaches us the importance of generosity and humility.

Kaph is associated with the secret power of creation, embodying the ability to mold the material world in accordance with divine will. The letter represents the power to shape one's reality, emphasizing how our thoughts and actions can profoundly affect the world around us. Kaph's numeric value is 20. It is a number that signifies redemption, a sense of purpose, and balanced spiritual growth.

Historically, Kaph's form is rooted in ancient Semitic scripts. Its open-handed design is thought to represent a protective hand or covering, suggesting protection and blessing from above. As a symbol of humility, it teaches that those who bend in reverence before a higher truth will find strength and purpose.

Final Kaph and its Meaning

The letter Kaph also has a special final form (ך), which is written when it appears at the end of a word. Unlike its regular form, which is bent, the final Kaph stands upright, symbolizing the transformation from humility to dignity. This shift in shape signifies that those who bow in humility and bend before higher wisdom will, in time, stand upright with confidence and integrity.

This upright form represents the spiritual journey of rising to fulfill divine standards and reveals that the ultimate power of Kaph is to gain the strength and ability to stand tall. It reinforces the principle that humility is a path to inner strength and that acts of kindness and generosity will ultimately lead to growth and recognition.

Interesting Fact

Kaph is associated with the 'crowning' of potential, where the potential is not only realized but also elevated to its highest form. This aspect of Kaph reflects its role in fostering spiritual and personal development, where the 'hand' that receives is also the one that crowns and completes the cycle of growth.

Kaph is associated with the concept of Keter (crown), one of the Sefirot in the Tree of Life. Kaph symbolizes the crown of creation, linking it to divine intention and wisdom. Its open hand shape represents the ability to receive and channel divine energy, making it a conduit for spiritual enlightenment.

The letter Kaph is prominent in the Priestly Blessing, a prayer of protection, grace, and peace. The knowledge of Kaph is believed to channel divine blessings to the community, reinforcing Kaph's role as a mediator between heaven and earth.

The straight and upright form of final Kaph (ך) is associated with unification and restoration. In some ancient texts, this form represents the coming together of separated elements to create a harmonious whole. It embodies the concept that through humility, one can bring together diverse aspects of life to achieve inner completeness and integrity.

Kaph is linked to the Kav HaMiddah (line of measurement). This concept ties Kaph to the principle of balance, suggesting that it embodies both the limits of the physical world and the infinite possibilities of spiritual growth. The letter Kaph thus holds the secret of measuring oneself against divine standards and finding one's place in the cosmic order.

In the Book of Psalms, the 119th chapter is an acrostic poem, with each stanza corresponding to a letter of the Hebrew alphabet. The section for Kaph emphasizes longing and seeking Yahweh's favor, underscoring the letter's symbolic relationship with prayer, humility, and the desire for spiritual fulfillment.

Spelling of Kaph

(Kaph, Peh)

"The Palm (Kaph) reveals through Speech (Peh)."

The Hebrew spelling of Kaph

Kaph (כ): Represents the palm or an open hand, symbolizing receptivity and the power to shape reality.

Peh (ף): This word signifies the mouth, representing the creative power of speech to manifest thoughts and intentions.

Together, these letters reveal that Kaph embodies the ability to shape the world through receptivity and clear communication.

Chapter Engagement

Meditating on Potential and Creation

Find a Calm Space: Sit comfortably in a quiet area, close your eyes, and take a few slow breaths. Inhale deeply through your nose and exhale through your mouth, allowing your body to relax.

Visualize Kaph: Imagine the letter Kaph in your mind as an open palm, cupping and holding a sphere of potential. See the sphere glowing brightly in your palm, representing the ability to shape intentions and bring them into reality.

Reflect on Receptivity: Contemplate how Kaph represents an open hand that receives and channels divine energy. What are you currently holding onto that could be shaped or shared for a higher purpose? How can you become more receptive to the blessings and wisdom available?

Channel Creative Energy: With each breath, visualize divine energy flowing into your open palm, filling it with light. Imagine this light transforming into words of kindness and positive intentions that you can speak into reality through Peh.

Set an Intention: Take a deep breath and set an intention to receive and share with an open palm. How can you use Kaph's receptive nature to shape your intentions into creative actions?

Return to Presence: Gradually open your eyes, grounded and centered. Carry this renewed sense of receptivity and creative potential into your day, nurturing positive intentions through clear communication.

CHAPTER 12

Lamed: The Tower of Learning

Lamed (ל)
Modern Hebrew Letter
The Modern form of Lamed is used in contemporary Hebrew.

Ancient Pictorial/Glyph: (A shepherd's staff or ox goad)

Ancient representation of Lamed symbolizes a disciple, one who is the teacher and the student (meaning learn and educate).

Introduction to Lamed

Explore the twelfth letter of the Hebrew aleph-beth: Lamed. Standing as the tallest letter in the Hebrew alphabet, Lamed reaches upward, symbolizing the aspiration towards higher wisdom and understanding. This letter embodies the heart of learning and teaching.

Name and Spellings

Lamed, often denoted as 'L,' represents the concept of learning and teaching in Hebrew. As you engage with Lamed, reflect on its pivotal role in guiding intellectual and spiritual growth.

Pronunciation Guide

Pronounced 'lah-med,' similar to the 'l' in 'look.' The articulation is clear and elevated, resonating with Lamed's stature as a symbol of authority and knowledge.

Corresponding Greek and English Letters

Lamed corresponds to the Greek Lambda (Λ, λ) and the English letter L. These counterparts share a commonality in their roles in phonetics and linguistics, often used to denote learning and literate abilities.

Numerical Value

Lamed represents the number 30. This number signifies a high level of spiritual and intellectual achievement, mirroring Lamed's association with the height of wisdom and accumulated learning.

Lamed as the Tower of Learning

Lamed's form, resembling a tower or a shepherd's staff, shows its function as a guide and protector of knowledge. The shape points upward, illustrating the relentless human pursuit of higher understanding and the divine. It serves as a metaphorical ox goad, steering thoughts and actions towards ethical and intellectual paths.

Spiritually, Lamed is considered a conduit between the earthly and the divine, facilitating the transmission of sacred teachings and divine will. It is the central letter in the Torah, emphasizing its role at the core of Judaic learning and spiritual life. Lamed teaches us about the responsibility that comes with knowledge: to lead, to guide, and to elevate others.

Lamed's presence in significant Hebrew words, like 'lev' (heart) and 'lamad' (to learn) underscores its foundational influence on emotional and intellectual development. It symbolizes the holistic approach to learning, where the acquisition of knowledge involves both the mind and the heart, leading to comprehensive personal growth.

Interesting Fact

Lamed is often seen as a bridge connecting the earthly to the heavenly. Its towering form is not just structural but symbolic, representing the ascent of prayers and spiritual yearnings toward higher realms. This vertical alignment highlights Lamed's role in spiritual ascension, making it a central figure in meditative and prayerful practices.

Lamed is the tallest letter in the Hebrew alphabet, extending above the line. This unique characteristic symbolizes its role as an exalted letter, often associated with striving towards and reaching for higher wisdom. This vertical extension is seen as a metaphorical ladder reaching toward the divine, illustrating the pursuit of spiritual ascension and enlightenment.

Lamed has a numerical value of 30, which symbolizes a state of balance and harmony. This balance is crucial in understanding and teaching, as it represents the equilibrium between receiving knowledge and imparting it. The number 30 is also linked to the 30 days of most months in the Hebrew calendar, suggesting a cycle of learning and renewal that refreshes and enriches human understanding regularly.

The word 'lev' (לב), meaning heart, starts with the letter Lamed. This positions Lamed as a symbol of intellectual knowledge, emotional intelligence, and understanding. The heart is considered the seat of wisdom in many spiritual traditions, showing that true knowledge involves both the mind and the emotions, reflecting Lamed's comprehensive influence.

Lamed is considered the central part of the Torah (the books of the Law), being the exact middle letter in the phrase that marks the center of the Torah scroll. This central placement underscores its importance in representing the heart of spiritual and moral law. It signifies the pivotal point of balance in the cosmic order, integrating spiritual laws with earthly existence.

Spelling of Lamed

(Lamed, Mem, Dalet)

"Guidance (Lamed) through Knowledge (Mem) leads to
a Doorway (Dalet)."

The Hebrew spelling of Lamed

ל מ ד

Lamed (ל): Represents guidance and learning, embodying the role of a teacher or leader.

Mem (מ): Symbolizes water and knowledge, reflecting depth, wisdom, and the flow of ideas.

Dalet (ד): Signifies a doorway, representing new beginnings and opportunities that arise through learning.

Together, these letters illustrate that Lamed facilitates a journey of knowledge and understanding, guiding one through doorways of new experiences and deeper insights.

Chapter Engagement: Lamed Meditation

Meditating on Balance and Ascent

Prepare Your Space: Find a quiet and comfortable spot where you can sit undisturbed. Settle into a comfortable seated position, either on a chair or on the floor, and gently close your eyes.

Ground Yourself: To center yourself, begin by taking a few deep breaths. Inhale deeply through your nose, allowing your abdomen to expand, and exhale slowly through your mouth. Repeat this a few times until you feel relaxed and present.

Visualize Lamed: In your mind's eye, picture the letter Lamed, tall and reaching upward beyond the other letters. Visualize it as a symbol of striving towards higher wisdom. See it extending upwards from a firm base, reaching towards the sky.

Reflect on Learning: Contemplate the role of Lamed as a guide in learning and leadership. Think about the areas in your life where you seek deeper understanding or where you could embody the qualities of a leader. What knowledge do you wish to ascend to, and what wisdom do you hope to attain?

Connect with the Heart: As Lamed also symbolizes the heart, focus on your heart center. Imagine a warm, glowing light in your chest that expands with each breath. Feel this light representing the emotional intelligence and compassion that Lamed encourages.

Set an Intention: As you continue to breathe deeply, set an intention related to balance and ascent. It might be achieving a better balance between your personal and professional life or striving to learn something new that elevates your understanding of the world.

Return and Reflect: Slowly bring your awareness back to the present moment. Take a few gentle breaths, and when you're ready, open your eyes. Consider writing down any insights or feelings that arose during your meditation. How can you apply the qualities of Lamed in your daily life?

CHAPTER 13

Mem: The Waters of Wisdom

Mem (מ,ם)
Modern Hebrew Letter

Modern Mem מ and its final form ם as used in contemporary Hebrew.

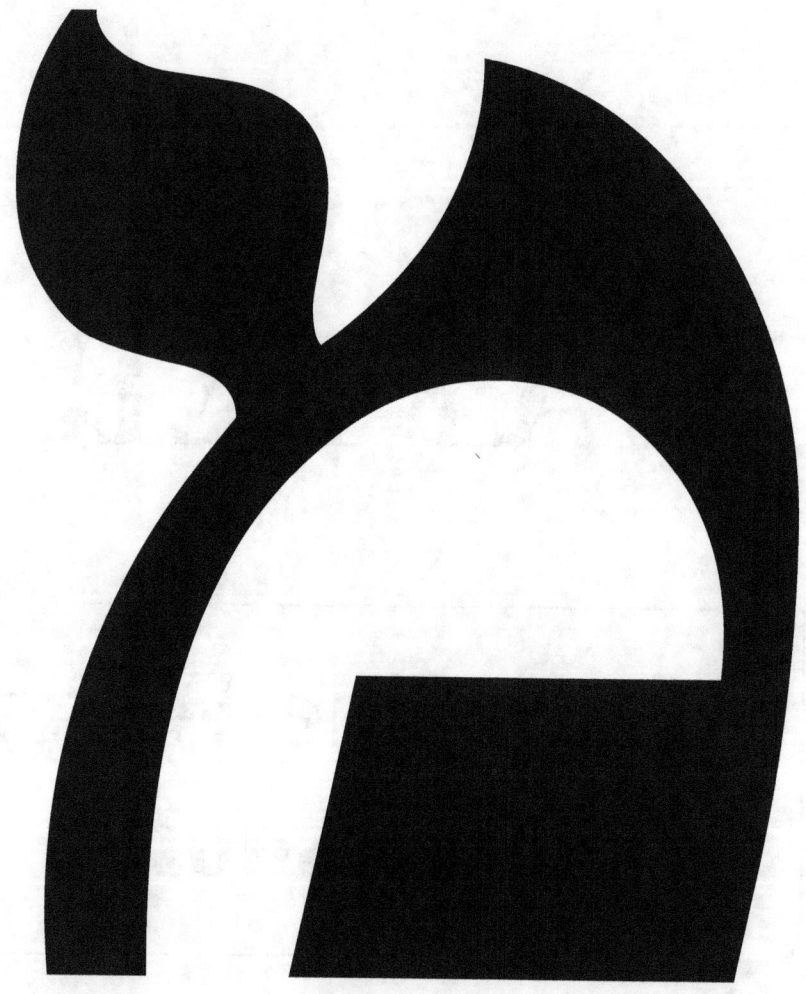

Ancient Pictorial/Glyph: (an image of water)

The ancient representation of Mem symbolizes fluid, water, and womb.

Introduction to Mem

Step into the depths of the Hebrew aleph-beth with Mem, the thirteenth letter. Mem represents water, the source of life and a symbol of wisdom and fluidity. This letter encourages exploration of the unconscious and the intuitive, reflecting the ebb and flow of emotions and ideas.

Name and Spellings

Mem, sometimes also spelled 'Mehm' and 'Mayim,' embodies the concepts of fluidity, life, and knowledge. As you delve into its nuances, consider its role in nourishing both the earth and the mind.

Pronunciation Guide

Pronounced 'mem,' similar to the 'm' in 'mother.' This soft, enveloping sound is reflective of Mem's symbolic association with water, encompassing and life-giving.

Corresponding Greek and English Letters

Mem corresponds to the Greek Mu (M, μ) and the English letter M. These letters play foundational roles in forming words across languages, symbolizing maternal and nurturing attributes often associated with water and life.

Numerical Value

In Hebrew numerology, Mem represents the number 40. This number often symbolizes periods of transformation and trial, such as the 40 days of rain during the flood and the 40 years the Israelites spent wandering in the desert. It reflects Mem's role in representing significant changes and transitions.

Mem as the Waters of Wisdom

Mem's form evokes an image of waves or undulating waters, representing the fluid and all-encompassing nature of water. This element is essential for life, making Mem a symbol of not just physical sustenance but also of spiritual and intellectual nourishment. Water's capacity to flow and adapt, to carve landscapes and sustain ecosystems, parallels the way thoughts and wisdom spread and influence cultures and individuals.

Spiritually, Mem symbolizes the deep wells of the unconscious, where intuition and profound insights reside. It invites us to dive into our inner depths, exploring the undercurrents of our psyche and the flowing rhythm of our emotions. This exploration can lead to revelations and personal growth. As water shapes stones, so does persistent study shape understanding. Mem's presence in the word 'mayim' (water) and 'mishnah' (repetition or study) underlines its significance in learning and spiritual practice. It encourages the continuous flow of learning, like water, which refreshes and revitalizes the spirit.

Mem is the Portal of Transformation. It is shaped like a wave and symbolizes the cyclical and transformative power of water, which is ever-changing yet constant. This dual nature mirrors the human journey through life's various phases. Water's ability to change states from ice to liquid to vapor parallels our own potential for transformation at different stages of life. Just as water cycles from the heavens to the earth and back again, so too does Mem remind us of the soul's cyclic journey from the spiritual to the physical realm and its eventual return.

Mem is often considered a mystical gate between different dimensions of existence. Its form, resembling an open or closed mouth, serves as a metaphorical portal that mediates between silence and expression, the seen and unseen, the known and the mysterious. This gate can be seen as a point of exchange where divine wisdom is communicated to the human world, and human experiences are translated back into spiritual lessons. The open and closed forms of Mem (מ and ם) suggest the dynamic between revelation and concealment, where some truths are revealed while others remain hidden, awaiting the right moment or level of understanding.

Mem's connection to the creative force of water extends to the realm of creativity and the arts. In many cultures, water is associated with creativity because of its flowing, adaptable nature that can carve new paths and bring nourishment to barren places. Thus, Mem encourages not only intellectual and spiritual fluidity but also creativity in expressing one's innermost thoughts and emotions. It nurtures the artist within, facilitating the flow of ideas and inspiring innovation in thought and action.

Finally, Mem's linkage to the word "memory" (which shares etymological roots with water in various languages) underscores its association with "time and recollection." Memory, like water, is fluid—constantly reshaped by the currents of our experiences and insights. This aspect of Mem suggests a deep well of ancestral and collective memory that nourishes our present understanding and connects us to past generations, flowing through time like a river through landscapes.

Interesting Fact

The final form of Mem, known as Mem sofit (ם), is always written in a closed loop and appears only at the end of words. This unique aspect is interpreted to represent the "closed waters," symbolizing hidden or esoteric wisdom that is not readily accessible to the uninitiated. In contrast, the open form of Mem (מ) symbolizes "revealed waters," referring to knowledge that is accessible and understandable to all. This distinction illustrates the dual nature of wisdom: some truths are open and clear, while others require deeper, more introspective inquiry to uncover.

Mem and the Divine Feminine: In Kabbalistic thought, Mem is often associated with the divine feminine aspect of Yahweh, known as the Shekhinah. This association is tied to the nurturing and life-giving properties of water, which is crucial for all life forms. Mem's linkage with the Shekhinah emphasizes its role in creation and sustenance, reflecting the nurturing aspect of the divine that is often characterized as feminine. This connection also highlights the protective and encompassing nature of the divine, much like the womb, which is symbolically represented by the enclosed form of Mem.

Spelling Mem (Mem, Yod, Mem Sofit)

"The Waters of Wisdom (Mem, also spelled 'Mayim,')
infused with Divine Insight (Yod) nourish and refresh (Mem)."

The Hebrew Spelling of Mem

מים

Mem (מ): Represents water, symbolizing wisdom, flexibility, and the flow of life. It embodies the ability to adapt and transform, deeply influencing both the natural world and human thought.

Yod (י): Symbolizes a divine spark or point of light, often associated with creativity and spiritual insight. In the context of Mayim, it connects the two Mems, illustrating the continuous flow and divine influence within the waters of wisdom.

Mem Sofit (ם): Also symbolizes nourishment and refreshment, highlighting its capacity to rejuvenate and renew the spirit and mind through continuous learning and growth.

Together, these aspects of Mem emphasize its role in sustaining intellectual and spiritual vitality, fostering a cycle of learning and renewal. The inclusion of Yod within Mayim further underscores the divine connection and the transformative power of wisdom and knowledge.

Chapter Engagement: Mem Meditation

Meditating on Fluidity and Renewal

Prepare Your Space: Choose a quiet, comfortable spot where you can sit undisturbed for a few minutes. Sit in a relaxed position, close your eyes, and begin to focus on your breathing. Take slow, deep breaths to center your thoughts and calm your body.

Visualize Mem: In your mind's eye, envision the letter Mem as a flowing body of water, such as a river or a gentle stream. See it moving smoothly and continuously, reflecting the light and adapting effortlessly to the contours of the land.

Contemplate Water's Qualities: Think about the qualities of water — its adaptability, its persistence, and its necessity for life. Reflect on how water nourishes and sustains all it touches. Consider how you can embody these qualities in your own life — flowing around obstacles, adapting to new situations, and nurturing growth in yourself and others.

Connect with Inner Wisdom: As you meditate on the image of flowing water, imagine that water as the flow of wisdom through your life. Visualize this wisdom, refreshing your mind, soothing your emotions, and invigorating your spirit. Think about specific areas in your life where this flow of wisdom could bring renewal and positive change.

Set an Intention: As you continue to breathe deeply, set a personal intention related to Mem's qualities. Perhaps you wish to become more adaptable, nurture your relationships more, or find new ways to refresh your spirit. Hold this intention in your mind as you breathe.

Slowly Return: Gradually bring your focus back to your physical surroundings. Wiggle your fingers and toes, stretch if you need to, and open your eyes when you're ready. Take a moment to reflect on your meditation and how you can carry forward the insights and intentions into your daily life.

CHAPTER 14

Nun: The Faithful Fish

Nun (נ,ן)
Modern Hebrew Letter

Modern Nun נ and its final form ן is used in contemporary Hebrew.

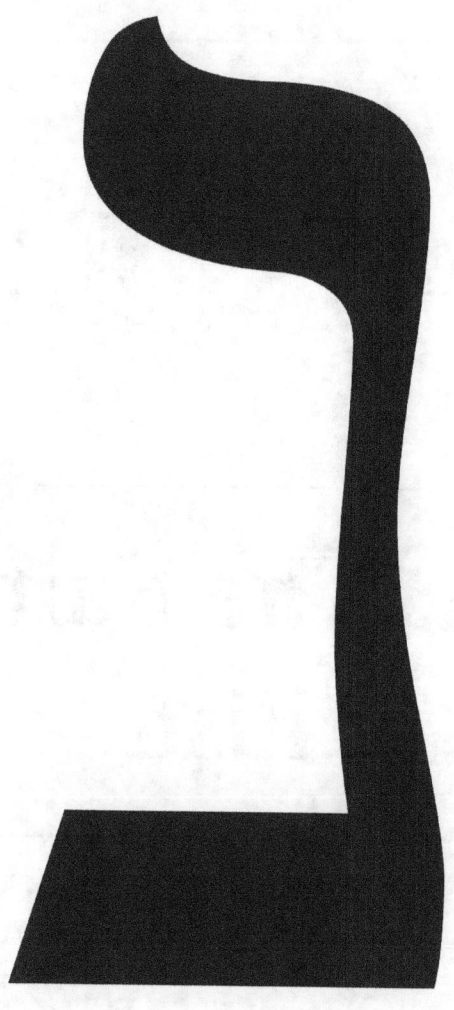

Ancient Pictorial/Glyph: (a fish)

The ancient representation of the Nun symbolizes a fish, sprout, and regeneration.

Introduction to Nun

Embark on the exploration of Nun, the fourteenth letter of the Hebrew aleph-beth. Symbolizing life, fertility, and movement, Nun reflects the dynamic and perpetuating aspects of existence, much like the ever-moving fish in the waters.

Name and Spellings

Nun, occasionally spelled as 'Noun,' captures themes of continuity and propagation. As we examine Nun, consider its embodiment of life's cyclical and progressive traits.

Pronunciation Guide

Pronounced 'noon,' similar to the 'n' in 'noon.' The sound is smooth and continuous, resonating with Nun's association with ongoing life cycles and movement.

Corresponding Greek and English Letters

Nun corresponds to the Greek Nu (N, ν), and the English letter N. Nun is integral in forming words and concepts and plays a vital role in the structure of language.

Numerical Value

Nun represents the number 50. This number symbolizes freedom and liberation. It reflects Nun's thematic ties to life, emerging into new phases of spiritual and existential freedom.

Nun as the Faithful Fish

The letter Nun's shape mimics the bending motion of a fish, symbolizing fertility, life, and the underlying currents that propel existence forward. This imagery underscores Nun's role in symbolizing the soul's journey through the material world—fluid, adaptive, and continuously evolving.

Spiritually, Nun represents faithfulness and the life force that sustains creation. Just as fish are often unseen beneath the surface of the water, so too are many of life's most vital processes, which are hidden from view but essential for the continuation of life. Nun encourages a deeper look into these hidden realms, promoting an understanding of the underlying forces at play in our lives and the universe.

Nun is seen as a symbol of humility and faith, often associated with the righteous falling and rising again, as expressed in Psalms 145:14. It embodies resilience and the perpetual motion required to navigate life's challenges, always striving towards growth and renewal.

Nun is the Eternal Cycle. The nun, representing the fish, encapsulates the themes of not only life and fertility but also the cyclical nature of existence. This connection is deepened by its numerical value of fifty, which in Jewish tradition is associated with the Jubilee year—a time of liberation and renewal that occurs every fifty years. This period marks the freeing of slaves and the restoration of land to its original owners, symbolizing a return to equilibrium and the restoration of balance in society.

Mystical Dimensions of Nun

In mystical Judaism, particularly in Kabbalistic thought, Nun is associated with the Neshama, the higher soul that embodies the divine spark within each person. This aspect of the soul is linked to higher consciousness and moral integrity, guiding individuals toward their spiritual purpose. The fish-like movement of the Nun, moving through the water effortlessly, is seen as a metaphor for the soul's navigation through the spiritual currents of the universe, always adapting yet remaining true to its divine essence.

Nun relates to the Messiah. Nun also holds a prophetic significance in Jewish eschatology. The term "Nun" appears in the messianic title "Ben David," which includes the letter Nun at the end of the Hebrew word for 'son' (Ben). The Nun as Ben signifies the perpetual legacy of David as it continues through the Messiah, who is believed to bring about a new era of peace and divine connection. The letter's form, bent as if in motion, symbolizes the active waiting and preparation that characterizes the Jewish people's anticipation of the messianic age.

Moreover, the letter Nun is said to encapsulate the entire cosmic struggle between good and evil. Its shape suggests dynamism and resilience, echoing the eternal fight against chaos represented in many spiritual traditions by the sea—a realm often associated with both life and danger. Nun's association with fish, creatures that can thrive in such a chaotic environment, symbolizes the ability to maintain one's purity and purpose despite the surrounding tumult.

Interesting Fact

Nun is connected to the concept of 'nes' (miracle), hinting at the miraculous nature of everyday existence and survival. This connection highlights the extraordinary within the ordinary, urging recognition of the miraculous in daily life and the spiritual lessons it offers.

Symbol of Perpetual Motion: In the context of the Torah's text, the letter Nun is unique in its presentation. In Numbers 10:35-36, the Nun appears inverted at the beginning and end of these verses, which are prayers recited as the Ark of the Covenant was carried. The inverted Nuns create a marker or parenthesis, suggesting that the verses are a significant and distinct message within the Torah. This unusual usage symbolizes the eternal nature of the journey, not just through the desert but through life and spiritual seeking. The inverted Nun emphasizes the idea of cyclical and ongoing divine guidance and protection, representing a perpetual state of spiritual movement and progression.

Nun and the Hidden Light: In deeper mystical teachings, Nun is connected to the concept of the "hidden light" of creation, an ancient light that was reserved by Yahweh for the righteous in the world to come. This light, created at the beginning of time, was hidden away after the first day due to its precious nature. The letter Nun, associated with faithfulness and the eternal soul, is thought to be a vessel for this light, embodying the potential for spiritual enlightenment and ultimate redemption that lies within each person. The association with fish, creatures that thrive in the depths, further emphasizes Nun's role as a bearer of deep, concealed wisdom.

The spelling of Nun (Nun, Wav, Nun)

"The Faithful Fish (Nun) connects (Wav) through
Perpetual Motion (Nun)."

The Hebrew spelling of

נ ו ן

Nun (נ): Represents the fish, symbolizing life, fertility, and the ability to navigate through the currents of life with agility and faith.

Wav (ו): Symbolizes connection, linking the spiritual and material realms and facilitating the flow of divine energy.

Final Nun (ן): This word signifies endurance and the continuation of the journey, reflecting the ongoing cycle of life and spiritual evolution.

Together, these letters embody the essence of Nun as a dynamic force of faith and resilience, continuously moving and adapting within the flow of life.

Chapter Engagement: Nun Meditation

Meditating on Resilience and Hidden Depths

1. **Prepare Your Space:** It is important to find a quiet and comfortable place where you can sit without any disturbances. To start, settle yourself into a relaxed yet upright position. Close your eyes and shift your attention solely to your breath and breathing. Take deep, slow breaths to center yourself and calm your mind.

2. **Visualize Nun:** Imagine the letter Nun in your mind as a gently swimming fish, moving effortlessly through the water. Picture this fish navigating with grace and ease, reflecting the resilience and adaptability symbolized by Nun.

3. **Contemplate Hidden Strengths:** Think about the hidden strengths and depths within you, much like the unseen life beneath the water's surface. Reflect on the internal resources you have that help you navigate through life's challenges, adapting and evolving as necessary.

4. **Embrace Resilience:** As you continue to breathe deeply, focus on the concept of resilience represented by Nun. Consider how, just like a fish swimming against the current, you have the power to overcome obstacles, rise, and keep moving forward.

5. **Set an Intention:** With each inhale, draw in strength and resilience; with each exhale, release fears and doubts. Set an intention to tap into your hidden depths and use your inner strength to propel you through any challenges you face.

6. **Return to Presence:** Slowly bring your awareness back to your physical surroundings. Wiggle your fingers and toes, stretch if needed, and when ready, open your eyes. Carry the sense of deep resilience and adaptability with you, ready to apply it to your day-to-day life.

CHAPTER 15

Samekh: The Upholding Support

Samekh (ס)
Modern Hebrew Letter
(Include image of modern Samekh ס)

Modern Samekh is used in contemporary Hebrew.

Ancient Pictorial/Glyph: (a prop or support)

Samekh is known for symbolizing a prop or support.

Introduction to Samekh

Venture into the fifteenth letter of the Hebrew aleph-beth: Samekh. This circular letter symbolizes support and protection, reflecting completeness and unity. It serves as a reminder of the divine support that upholds the universe and sustains us.

Name and Spellings

Samekh, occasionally spelled 'Samech,' embodies the concepts of support and prop. As you explore Samekh, reflect on its pivotal role in providing stability and protection in the Hebrew language and spirituality.

Pronunciation Guide

Pronounced 'sah-mehk,' with a soft 's' sound similar to the 's' in 'sun.' The pronunciation is clear and strong, echoing Samekh's association with strength and stability.

Corresponding Greek and English Letters

Samekh has no direct counterpart in Greek but resembles the English letter S in form and sound. It holds a significant role in forming words and sentences in the Hebrew language.

Numerical Value

In Hebrew numerology, Samekh represents the number 60. This number often signifies support and protection, mirroring Samekh's symbolic role in providing structure and upholding divine and universal principles.

Samekh as the Upholding Support

Samekh's form is circular, visually resembling a wheel or a circle that supports and upholds everything within its circumference. This completeness illustrates Samekh's primary function of support. It is the prop or pillar that stands firm, providing stability to everything that rests upon it.

Spiritually, Samekh is seen as a reflection of the divine support that sustains creation and guides the journey of the soul. In Kabbalistic thought, Samekh represents the omnipresence of divine protection, the unseen pillar that upholds the fragile structure of life. It teaches us about the importance of balance and how a supportive framework is essential for the stability of the body, mind, and spirit.

Furthermore, Samekh is associated with the concept of cycles and continuity, like a wheel that never ceases to turn. It reminds us that divine guidance and protection are ever-present, providing strength through life's ups and downs.

Cosmic Cycle and Renewal: Samekh's circular shape also symbolizes the cycle of renewal and regeneration. It embodies the concept of the ouroboros, the ancient symbol of a serpent eating its own tail, which represents the endless cycle of creation and destruction, life and death, and perpetual renewal. In this cosmic dance, Samekh reminds us of the constant flux of the universe and our role within it—continuously evolving, growing, and transforming. This perpetual motion mirrors the cycles of the seasons, the orbits of the planets, and the rhythmic patterns of life itself, suggesting that stability often depends not on stasis but on the harmony of constant motion.

Personal Resilience and Support: On a personal level, Samekh encourages an introspective look at how we support ourselves and others. It asks us to consider the foundations upon which we build our lives and challenges us to be the supportive pillars for others. Just as Samekh acts as a prop or support, it inspires us to be resilient and reliable, to be the emotional and spiritual backbone for those in need. This letter's essence teaches that true strength is found in the ability to uphold others, fostering a community where mutual support and understanding prevail and where every individual can find the strength to stand firm against the challenges of life.

Interesting Fact

Samekh is the only fully enclosed letter in the Hebrew alphabet, reinforcing its symbolism of protection and containment. It is associated with the divine support provided to those who falter, symbolizing the safety net catching those who stumble.

Symbolic Structure and Stability: Samekh's circular form is unique among Hebrew letters, which typically feature angular shapes. This roundness symbolizes perfection, completeness, and the stability inherent in circles. Intriguingly, the Talmud relates a legend that the letter Samekh supported the fallen walls of Jerusalem, standing miraculously. This story highlights Samekh's role as a symbol of divine support and protection, even amidst destruction, reflecting its metaphysical role as a sustainer of spiritual and physical realms.

Astronomical Association: In ancient Jewish astrology, Samekh is associated with the planet Saturn, known in Hebrew as 'Shabbatai' (the seventh planet). Saturn, often epicted in astrological traditions as the great regulator and bearer of time, parallels Samekh's themes of cycles, limits, and divine justice. This connection underscores the role of Samekh in maintaining cosmic order, embodying the structure and discipline necessary to uphold the universe's laws and cycles.

Spelling of Samekh (Samekh, Mem, Kaph)

"The Supportive Circle (Samekh) nourishes (Mem) with protection (Kaph)."

The Hebrew spelling of

ס מ ך

Samekh (ס): Represents a circle or wheel, symbolizing continuous support and the unending cycle of life.

Mem (מ): Symbolizes water, conveying nourishment and life-giving sustenance that flows within the supportive bounds of Samekh.

Kaph (ך): Signifies the palm of a hand, embodying protection and the ability to hold or encompass safely within its grasp.

Together, these letters illustrate Samekh's function as a sustaining force, providing nourishment and protection within the cycles of existence.

Chapter Engagement: Samekh Meditation

Meditating on Support and Continuity

1. **Prepare Your Space:** Find a quiet, comfortable place where you can sit undisturbed. Sit in a relaxed but upright position, close your eyes, and begin to focus on your breathing. Take deep, slow breaths to center yourself and calm your mind.

2. **Visualize Samekh:** Imagine the letter Samekh in your mind as a perfect circle or wheel. Visualize this circle as strong and supportive, spinning slowly and steadily. See it glowing with a warm, protective light, encompassing everything within its circumference.

3. **Contemplate Support:** Think about the ways Samekh represents support and protection in your life. Reflect on the structures or people that provide you with stability. Consider how you can embody the qualities of Samekh by offering support and strength to others.

4. **Embrace Continuity:** As you meditate on the continuous motion of the Samekh, contemplate the cycles in your own life. Recognize the flow of beginnings and endings, challenges, and resolutions. Feel reassured by the continuity that Samekh symbolizes—nothing is static, and each phase of life contributes to growth and understanding.

5. **Set an Intention:** With each inhale, draw in strength and stability from the supportive energy of Samekh. With each exhale, release any fears or doubts that hinder your sense of security. Set a personal intention to foster stability and continuity, both within yourself and in your interactions with the world.

6. **Return to Presence:** Gradually bring your focus back to your physical surroundings. Wiggle your fingers and toes, stretch if needed, and when ready, open your eyes. Take a moment to reflect on your meditation and how you can apply the insights and intentions to your daily life.

CHAPTER 16

Ayin: The Eye of Understanding

Ayin (ע)
Modern Hebrew Letter

Modern Ayin is used in contemporary Hebrew.

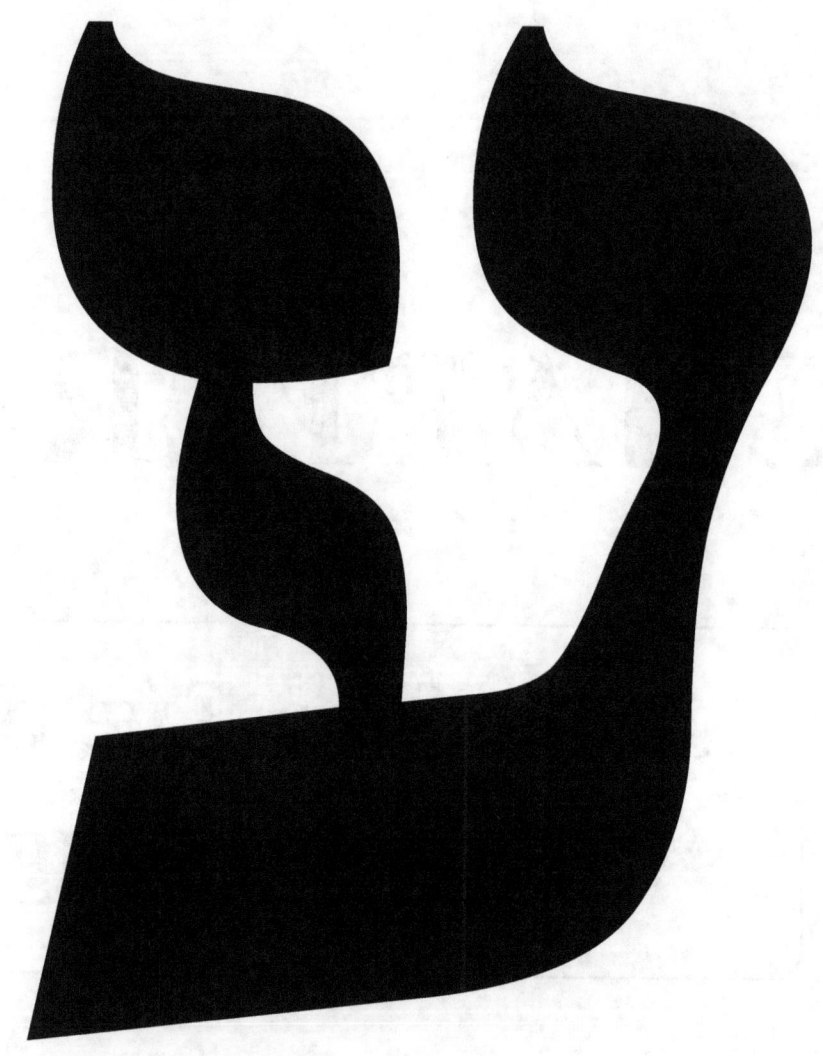

Ancient Pictorial/Glyph: (an eye)

The ancient representation of Ayin is symbolized as an eye.

Introduction to Ayin

Explore the sixteenth letter of the Hebrew aleph-beth: Ayin. This letter symbolizes the eye, representing perception and understanding. It encourages seeing beyond the surface and gaining insight into the deeper truths that shape the world.

Name and Spellings

Ayin, sometimes spelled 'Ain,' embodies the concept of sight and perception. As you explore Ayin, reflect on its role in providing clarity and insight, both in language and spiritual understanding.

Pronunciation Guide

It is pronounced 'ah-yeen,' with a soft guttural sound that is challenging to replicate in English. The sound is closer to the Arabic 'ayn' and carries an ancient resonance of depth and wisdom.

Corresponding Greek and English Letters

Ayin corresponds to the Greek Omicron (O, o) and the English letter O. Although different in pronunciation, these letters play significant roles in forming the structure of words and language.

Numerical Value

In Hebrew numerology, Ayin represents the number 70. This number is often associated with a multitude of perspectives and understanding, representing the 70 elders of Israel and the 70 languages of the world.

Ayin as the Eye of Understanding

Ayin's form visually resembles an eye or a circle, emphasizing its symbolic connection to sight and awareness. As an eye, Ayin invites us to perceive the unseen and recognize the hidden layers of reality that lie just below the surface.

Spiritually, Ayin symbolizes deeper spiritual understanding and the ability to see beyond illusions to the truths that shape existence. Ayin reflects the divine eye that oversees and understands all things, acting as a window through which divine knowledge flows into the world. It challenges us to open our inner vision, illuminating our minds with the clarity of wisdom and understanding.

Furthermore, Ayin's connection to the number 70 reveals its comprehensive nature. It invites us to embrace multiple perspectives and understand how diverse viewpoints can contribute to a fuller, more complete understanding of the world. In this way, Ayin embodies an eye that perceives unity in diversity, finding harmony among differences.

Ayin acts as an eye of understanding and as a gateway to higher consciousness. Its shape and symbolic role as an observer encourages self-analysis and self-awareness. By meditating on Ayin, individuals are invited to explore the depths of their own psyche, unveiling subconscious patterns and hidden truths. This introspective journey facilitated by Ayin aids in personal growth and spiritual awakening. It enables individuals to connect more deeply with their inner selves and the surrounding universe.

Ayin represents judgment and discernment. Ayin is the ability to "see" clearly, which is linked to making wise decisions and discerning right from wrong. This aspect of Ayin emphasizes its importance in leadership and governance, where clear vision and moral insight are paramount. Ayin provides the discernment necessary to navigate the moral difficulties of life, encouraging a balanced and ethical approach to personal and communal challenges.

Interesting Fact

Ayin is considered the eye of divine providence, symbolizing Yahweh's all-seeing presence in the world. It represents the window to the spiritual realm and the passage through which divine light illuminates human consciousness.

Ayin is often associated with the concept of duality and the choices that shape our reality. The letter Ayin means **"eye,"** which symbolizes perception and insight. However, it also represents the idea of seeing both good and evil in the world, embodying the dual nature of existence. This duality emphasizes the power of choice and the moral responsibility that comes with the ability to see and understand the difficulties of life. By recognizing the dual aspects of creation, one can make informed decisions that align with spiritual growth and divine will.

Ayin is connected to the **"Ohr HaGanuz,"** or the Hidden Light, which is said to be a primordial light created by God on the first day of creation. This light was hidden away for the righteous in the future world, but it is believed that remnants of this light can be accessed through deep spiritual practice and meditation. Ayin, as the "eye," is seen as a vessel through which one can perceive glimpses of this Hidden Light, gaining profound insights and spiritual illumination that transcend ordinary perception.

Spelling Ayin (Ayin, Yod, Nun)

"The Eye (Ayin) of Divine Wisdom (Yod) leads to Spiritual Continuity (Nun)."

The Hebrew spelling of Ayin

עין

Ayin (ע): Represents the eye or insight.

Yod (י): Symbolizes divine wisdom or the hand of God.

Nun (ן): Reflects spiritual continuity or faithfulness.

In this combination, Ayin embodies the profound connection between divine insight, wisdom, and the enduring nature of spiritual truth.

Chapter Engagement: Ayin Meditation

Meditating on Insight and Perception

1. **Prepare Your Space:** Find a quiet, comfortable place where you can sit undisturbed. Sit in a relaxed but upright position, close your eyes, and begin to focus on your breathing. Take deep, slow breaths to center yourself and calm your mind.

2. **Visualize Ayin:** Imagine the letter Ayin in your mind as a radiant eye. See this eye-opening, releasing a gentle light that illuminates everything it sees. This light symbolizes divine insight and the ability to perceive deeper truths.

3. **Contemplate Perception:** Think about the ways in which you perceive the world around you. Reflect on perception's dual nature—the ability to see both the physical and the spiritual, the good and the bad. Consider how Ayin invites you to look beyond the surface and understand the hidden layers of reality.

4. **Connect with the Divine Insight:** As you focus on Ayin, imagine its light revealing the hidden aspects of your life and the world. Feel this light as a source of wisdom and clarity, helping you to see through illusions and understand the true nature of things. This insight connects you to the divine, allowing you to align your perception with higher truths.

5. **Set an Intention:** With each inhale, draw in the clarity and insight of Ayin; with each exhale, release confusion and superficial judgments. Set a personal intention to use this divine perception to guide your thoughts, actions, and decisions. Commit to looking beyond the obvious and seeking the deeper meaning in your experiences.

6. **Return to Presence:** Gradually bring your focus back to your physical surroundings. Wiggle your fingers and toes, stretch if needed, and when ready, open your eyes. Take a moment to reflect on your meditation and how you can apply the insights and intentions to your daily life.

CHAPTER 17

Peh: The Mouth of Expression

Peh (פ,ף)
Modern Hebrew Letter

Modern Peh פ and its final form ף are used in contemporary Hebrew.

Ancient Pictorial/Glyph: (a mouth)

Ancient representation of Peh symbolizes a mouth as in speech.

Introduction to Peh

Venture into the seventeenth letter of the Hebrew aleph-beth: Peh. This letter symbolizes the mouth, representing speech, expression, and communication. It embodies the creative power of words and the ability to influence and shape reality through speech.

Name and Spellings

Peh, sometimes also spelled **'Peh' or 'Feh,'** embodies the concept of communication. As you delve into Peh, reflect on the power of words and how they can build, destroy, heal, and transform.

Pronunciation Guide

Pronounced **'pay,'** similar to the **'p'** in **'pen.'** Without the dagesh **(dot)** in the center, it's pronounced **'fay,'** like the **'f'** in **'fun.'** The versatility of this letter echoes its role in influencing meaning through subtle changes in pronunciation.

Corresponding Greek and English Letters

Peh corresponds to the Greek Pi (Π, π) and the English letter P. Both are foundational letters that form words, making them integral to language.

Numerical Value

In Hebrew numerology, Peh represents the number 80. This number symbolizes strength and completion, reflecting the power of Peh to influence through speech, offering a path to fulfillment.

Peh as the Mouth of Expression

Peh's form resembles a mouth, emphasizing its symbolic connection to communication and speech. The mouth serves as a gateway for expression, revealing the inner thoughts and intentions of a person. Peh encourages us to use words mindfully, recognizing the creative and transformative power they hold.

Spiritually, Peh represents the divine aspect of speech, where words become vessels for the transmission of sacred ideas and truths. In Kabbalistic thought, Peh signifies the ability to manifest the divine will through language, reminding us that our words can shape reality by influencing thoughts and actions.

Peh's presence in words like 'poh' (here) and 'peh' (mouth) emphasizes the importance of being present and using our speech purposefully. The dual pronunciation of Peh—with and without the dagesh—mirrors the balance between giving and receiving, creation and destruction. This dual nature serves as a reminder that words can both build and break down, urging careful consideration of what we express.

Peh as a Portal of Creation and Revelation Peh not only acts as the mouth of expression but also as a portal through which hidden thoughts and spiritual insights are revealed to the world. This gateway is not just about articulating thoughts but also about unveiling deeper truths that can be transformative. In mystical traditions, Peh is seen as a channel for prophecy and divine revelation, where the sacred breath animates the letters to convey profound spiritual messages. This aspect of Peh underscores the sacred responsibility that comes with speech—the power to disclose truths that can enlighten minds and elevate souls.

Peh is the power of naming. The act of naming is both a form of creation and a means of exerting influence over the material world. Peh, which symbolizes the mouth, is directly connected to this concept. It is through Peh that names are given, defining the essence and influencing the fate of the named. This power is evident in biblical narratives where Yahweh names the celestial bodies, and Adam names the animals, establishing dominion and understanding through the act of naming. Peh thus embodies the creative potential that lies in defining and describing the world around us, reminding us of the profound impact our words have on our environment.

Peh challenges us to consider the ethical dimensions of our speech. In Hebrew law, much emphasis is placed on the ethics of speech, such as avoiding gossip (lashon hara) and speaking truthfully. In Jewish law, much emphasis is placed on the ethics of speech, such as avoiding gossip (lashon hara) and speaking truthfully. Peh embodies this moral framework, urging us to use our words to uplift rather than harm, to unite rather than divide, and to enlighten rather than obscure.

Peh in Artistic Expression Beyond verbal communication, Peh extends to all forms of expression that emerge from the 'mouth' of creativity. These expressions include singing, poetry, and other forms of artistic expression where the voice and words play a central role. Peh symbolizes artistic expression as a reflection of the soul's language, where emotions and thoughts are conveyed not just through words but through the rhythm, tone, and emotion of the artistic medium.

Interesting Fact

Peh is associated with the divine act of creation, where Yahweh speaks the universe into existence. The letter thus represents the creative force of speech and its ability to manifest divine intentions in the material world.

Peh and the Sefer Yetzirah

In the ancient Jewish text, the Sefer Yetzirah (Book of Formation), which discusses the mysticism behind Hebrew letters and the creation of the universe, Peh is associated with the planet Mars. This connection is significant because Mars in Jewish astrology symbolizes energy, strength, and sometimes conflict. This association reflects the intense power of Peh as a vehicle for speech and expression, capable of invoking strong reactions and movements akin to the assertive and forceful energies of Mars. The alignment of Peh with Mars highlights the dual capacity of speech to instigate change and confront challenges, emphasizing the transformative power of words.

Peh is unique among the Hebrew letters in that it has two forms: one with a dot (dagesh) in the middle, known as Peh, and one without, known as Fe. Intriguingly, the dagesh in the center of Peh is said to symbolize a hidden spark or seed of truth that is protected within the letter. This hidden dot signifies the essence of insight and wisdom that is often concealed within words and must be discerned with careful attention. In Kabbalistic thought, this hidden aspect of Peh suggests that the deepest truths require introspection and insight to uncover, much like the seed that holds the potential for life within its core, hidden until the conditions are right for its expression.

Spelling of Peh (Peh, Yod, Aleph)

"The Mouth of Expression (Peh) manifests (Yod) the
Divine Essence (Aleph)."

The Hebrew spelling of

פ י א

Peh (פ): Represents the mouth, symbolizing communication and the power of expression.

Yod (י): Symbolizes manifestation, acting as a divine spark that brings ideas and speech into reality.

Aleph (א): Represents the divine essence underlying all creation and speech, imbuing words with deeper spiritual significance.

Together, these letters illustrate Peh's role as a conduit for bringing forth divine insight into the world through the power of speech, emphasizing the creative and transformative potential of words.

Chapter Engagement: Peh Meditation

Meditating on Expression and Manifestation

1. **Prepare Your Space:** Find a quiet, comfortable place where you can sit undisturbed. Sit in a relaxed but upright position, close your eyes, and begin to focus on your breathing. Take deep, slow breaths to center yourself and calm your mind.

2. **Visualize Peh:** Imagine the letter Peh in your mind as a mouth opening to speak. Visualize this mouth as a channel through which thoughts and feelings are expressed. See the mouth glowing with a soft light, representing the divine spark (Yod) that infuses your words with power and purpose.

3. **Contemplate Expression:** Think about the ways in which you use your voice and words in daily life. Reflect on how your speech can create, influence, and transform your reality and that of others. Consider the ethical implications of your words and how they can be used to uplift and inspire rather than harm or mislead.

4. **Connect with Divine Essence:** As you meditate on the image of Peh, contemplate how each word you speak carries a piece of the divine essence (Aleph). Feel the responsibility and power that comes with this understanding. Envision your words aligning with this higher purpose, becoming vessels for truth, kindness, and enlightenment.

5. **Set an Intention:** With each inhale, draw in clarity and purpose; with each exhale, release misunderstandings and negativity. Set a personal intention to use your power of speech to affect your world positively. Decide on one specific way you will use your words to make a constructive change or support someone today.

6. **Return to Presence:** Gradually bring your focus back to your physical surroundings. Wiggle your fingers and toes, stretch if needed, and when ready, open your eyes. Take a moment to reflect on your meditation and how you can apply the insights and intentions to your daily interactions.

CHAPTER 18

Tzaddi: The Righteous Path

Tzaddi (צ,ץ)
Modern Hebrew Letter

Modern Tzaddi צ and its final form ץ are used in contemporary Hebrew.

Ancient Pictorial/Glyph: (a man kneeling or a hook)

The ancient representation of Tzaddi symbolizes a man kneeling, a hook or a fishhook.

Introduction to Tzaddi

Explore the eighteenth letter of the Hebrew aleph-beth: Tzaddi. This letter symbolizes righteousness, humility, and the search for truth. It embodies the ideals of the tzaddik (righteous person) and the ethical journey toward spiritual wholeness.

Name and Spellings

Tzaddi, also spelled **'Tsadi,'** **'Tsade,'** and **'Tsaday,'** embodies concepts of justice and humility. As you explore Tzaddi, reflect on its role in guiding ethical behavior and the pursuit of a meaningful, truthful life.

Pronunciation Guide

Pronounced **'Za-day,'** 'sah-dee,' similar to the 'ts' in **'cats.'** The sound is distinctive and sharp, reflecting Tzaddi's association with clarity and directness in ethical and moral pursuits.

Corresponding Greek and English Letters

Tzaddi does not have a direct counterpart in Greek or English alphabets, highlighting its distinctive sound and meaning within Hebrew. Its unique nature underscores its spiritual significance.

Numerical Value

In Hebrew numerology, Tzaddi represents the number 90. This number is associated with humility and the elevation of consciousness, reflecting Tzaddi's role in facilitating spiritual growth and enlightenment.

Tzaddi as the Righteous Path

Tzaddi's form resembles a man kneeling, symbolizing humility and devotion, or a hook, which implies connection. This form emphasizes Tzaddi's primary function in symbolizing righteousness and the journey toward ethical and spiritual fulfillment.

Tzaddi represents the tzaddik (righteous person), who strives for integrity and embodies divine principles. In Kabbalistic thought, Tzaddi signifies the balance between justice and compassion, showing how to act with kindness while adhering to moral truths. The act of kneeling by the figure highlights the significance of humility in this journey, indicating the necessity of surrendering to higher principles, which is essential for one to walk a righteous path.

Tzaddi's association with hooks illustrates its role in connecting individuals to divine guidance. It invites us to seek out spiritual principles that elevate our lives and actions, allowing us to become conduits of goodness and justice in the world. The final form of Tzaddi (ץ) extends below the baseline, reflecting the deeply rooted nature of this letter's values.

Tzaddi is often portrayed as a guardian or keeper of sacred mysteries and deep spiritual truths. This role is symbolically represented by its form, which not only resembles a humble, kneeling figure but also can be seen as a vessel that safely contains and protects sacred knowledge. This aspect of Tzaddi underscores the need for a protective embrace around profound spiritual insights, ensuring they are not exposed prematurely or misunderstood. The guardianship by Tzaddi implies that true wisdom must be approached with reverence and readiness, only accessible to those who are spiritually prepared to receive it.

Tzaddi can also be interpreted as a symbol of ecological consciousness and the ethical stewardship of the Earth. The shape that mimics a hook or anchor suggests a deep connection to the Earth, rooting the spiritual journey in the physical world. This connection highlights the responsibility to safeguard and sustain the natural environment, drawing a parallel between the health of the planet and spiritual well-being. In this context, Tzaddi advocates for a harmonious balance between human actions and the natural world, urging us to consider the impact of our behaviors on the Earth's ecosystems.

Interesting Fact

In Jewish mystical teachings, Tzaddi symbolizes the power of the righteous to bring balance and harmony to the world. It is associated with the concept of 'tikkun olam,' or repairing the world, urging every individual to contribute positively to society by living ethically.

Tzaddi and the Cosmic Order: In Jewish mysticism, particularly within the framework of the Kabbalah, Tzaddi is associated with the sefirah of Netzach, which represents eternity, victory, and endurance. This connection underlines Tzaddi's role in the eternal struggle between good and evil, as well as its enduring nature in maintaining moral and spiritual order. The letter Tzaddi, embodying the righteous person, symbolizes the victory of spirit over matter, suggesting that true endurance in righteousness has the power to transcend earthly challenges and align with the divine cosmic order.

Symbolic Use in Sacred Texts: The placement of the letter Tzaddi within sacred texts holds special significance. It often marks passages that discuss the profound depths of Yahweh's judgment and mercy. For example, the book of Psalms uses Tzaddi prominently in verses that deal with justice and deliverance, aligning with its symbolic meaning of righteousness and divine connection. Additionally, in the intricate design of Torah scrolls, Tzaddi's unique form, particularly its final version that extends below the line, is carefully crafted to symbolize the depth of divine justice extending into the earthly realm, illustrating how divine laws penetrate and influence the material world.

Spelling of Tzaddi (Tzaddi, Samekh, Dalet)

"The Righteous Path (Tzaddi) supports (Samekh) justice (Dalet)."
The Hebrew spelling of Tzaddi is

צ ס ד

Tzaddi (צ): Symbolizes righteousness and the journey toward spiritual and ethical fulfillment.
Samekh (ס): Represents support, illustrating the necessary foundation that upholds the principles of righteousness.
Dalet (ד): Signifies a door or gateway, implying the access or transition to justice and moral integrity.

Together, these letters emphasize Tzaddi's role in fostering a supportive environment that nurtures the pursuit of justice and righteousness.

Chapter Engagement: Tzaddi Meditation

Meditating on Righteousness and Spiritual Growth

1. **Prepare Your Space:** Find a quiet, comfortable spot where you can sit undisturbed. Sit in a relaxed but upright position, close your eyes, and begin to focus on your breathing. Take deep, slow breaths to center yourself and calm your mind.

2. **Visualize Tzaddi:** Imagine the letter Tzaddi in your mind as a kneeling figure or a firmly anchored hook. Visualize it as a symbol of stability, righteousness, and connection to divine principles.

3. **Contemplate Righteousness:** Think about what righteousness means to you. Reflect on how you can embody these qualities in your daily life. Consider the areas where you could improve and the strengths you already possess that help you maintain ethical standards.

4. **Connect with Support:** As you meditate on Tzaddi, consider the supportive roles in your life. Think about how you support others and how you are supported. Acknowledge the importance of a strong foundation that helps you uphold your values and principles.

5. **Set an Intention:** With each inhale, draw in strength and stability from the energy of Tzaddi. With each exhale, release any fears or doubts that might hinder your path to spiritual and ethical growth. Set a personal intention to act with righteousness and justice, guiding your decisions and interactions.

6. **Return to Presence:** Gradually bring your focus back to your physical surroundings. Wiggle your fingers and toes, stretch if needed, and when ready, open your eyes. Take a moment to reflect on your meditation and how you can apply the insights and intentions to your daily life.

CHAPTER 19

Qoph: The Sacred Cycle

Qoph (ק)
Modern Hebrew Letter

Modern Qoph is used in contemporary Hebrew.

Ancient Pictorial/Glyph: (back of a head, a needle)

The ancient representation of Qoph symbolizes the back of a head or a needle.

Introduction to Qoph

Enter the nineteenth letter of the Hebrew aleph-beth: Qoph. This letter symbolizes cycles and holiness, representing both the sacredness of time and the search for truth. It bridges the gap between the mundane and the divine, connecting the earthly to the spiritual.

Name and Spellings

Qoph, sometimes spelled 'Kof,' embodies ideas of cycles, holiness, and search. As you explore Qoph, reflect on its significance as a letter that symbolizes the journey from the superficial to the profound.

Pronunciation Guide

Pronounced 'kof,' similar to the 'k' in 'kite.' The sound is firm and clear, signifying the distinctness of Qoph's purpose in guiding toward the path of holiness.

Corresponding Greek and English Letters

Qoph has no direct counterpart in Greek but is closest in sound to the English letter Q. Its distinctive pronunciation and symbolism make it a unique feature of the Hebrew alphabet.

Numerical Value

In Hebrew numerology, Qoph represents the number 100. This number is associated with completion, sanctification, and fulfillment, reflecting Qoph's role in transcending the mundane to achieve a higher spiritual state.

Qoph as the Sacred Cycle

Qoph's form, resembling the back of a head or a needle with a long tail, reflects the journey from material to spiritual realms. It signifies cycles of completion and the importance of holiness in all stages of life.

Qoph represents the quest for truth and the pursuit of spiritual growth. In Kabbalistic thought, Qoph signifies the circular nature of time and the perpetual cycles that shape existence. It encourages the examination of superficial perceptions to uncover the hidden sacredness in everyday life. The needle-like form of Qoph suggests the precision needed to navigate this journey and the ability to pierce through illusions to reach the divine.

Qoph's symbolism extends to represent the boundaries that separate the known from the unknown, the visible from the invisible. Its form, which curves to enclose a space while extending outward, symbolizes the horizon line that both encloses our visible world and hints at what lies beyond. This horizon metaphorically reflects the edge of human understanding and the divine mysteries that lie beyond human perception. Qoph challenges us to expand our awareness and push beyond our conventional boundaries, urging a deeper exploration of both the external universe and our internal spiritual landscapes.

Qoph is seen as representing the **"holy spark"** or the divine essence that resides within everyone. This interpretation is inspired by Qoph's association with the word "kadosh," meaning holy. The letter's shape, resembling a needle, is thought to symbolize the pinpoint precision and focus required to access and nurture this inner divinity. This perspective encourages introspection and meditation as means to connect with and enhance one's innermost sacred qualities. By focusing on the divine spark within, practitioners are believed to transcend mundane existence and achieve a higher state of spiritual purity and enlightenment.

Furthermore, Qoph's presence in words like 'Kadosh' (holy) and 'kuf' (monkey) shows its dual nature. While it can represent the pursuit of superficial desires, it ultimately signifies the aspiration to transcend them and attain holiness through spiritual discipline.

Interesting Fact

Qoph is said to represent the passage between night and day, bridging darkness and light. It encourages looking beyond appearances to find divine truths that connect all cycles and stages of life.

Qoph is associated with the back of the head, representing what is behind and unseen. This association extends to the celestial sphere, where Qoph is linked to the darkest part of the moon, the part that is never visible from Earth. This hidden aspect of the moon symbolizes the unseen mysteries of the universe and the subconscious mind, reflecting Qoph's role in exploring deep, hidden truths that are beyond ordinary perception. This connection illustrates how Qoph embodies the concept of the unknown and the mystical, encouraging a deeper dive into the spiritual mysteries that transcend our visible reality.

The placement of Qoph in sacred Hebrew texts often marks passages that delve into deep existential questions or that describe the transcendence from physical to spiritual realms. Qoph is the first letter of words that relate to holiness and separation, such as "qedushah" (holiness) and "qadosh" (holy), highlighting its importance in texts that explore sacredness and spiritual ascent. Moreover, the letter Qoph is traditionally believed to hold a protective power when used in amulets and talismans, particularly against evil spirits and negative forces, underscoring its role as a guardian of spiritual purity and integrity.

The spelling of Qoph (Qoph, Wav, Peh)

"The Needle of Insight (Qoph) connects (Wav) to the Mouth of Expression (Peh)."

The Hebrew spelling of Qoph is

ק ו פ

Qoph (ק): Represents the needle, symbolizing the ability to pierce through illusions to uncover deeper truths and the divine essence.

Wav (ו): Symbolizes connection, linking the deep insights gained through Qoph to the rest of existence.

Peh (פ): Signifies the mouth, representing expression and the articulation of the profound revelations and sacred wisdom uncovered by Qoph.

Together, these letters emphasize Qoph's role as a tool of spiritual discernment, bridging the gap between divine mysteries and their expression in the world.

Chapter Engagement: Qoph Meditation

Meditating on Depth and Insight

1. **Prepare Your Space:** Find a quiet, comfortable place where you can sit undisturbed. Sit in a relaxed but upright position, close your eyes, and begin to focus on your breathing. Take deep, slow breaths to center yourself and calm your mind.

2. **Visualize Qoph:** Imagine the letter Qoph in your mind as a needle, piercing through layers of illusion to reach deep truths. Visualize this needle as sharp and precise, glowing with a gentle light, symbolizing clarity and insight.

3. **Contemplate Insight:** Think about the areas in your life where you seek deeper understanding or where superficial perceptions may be limiting your view. Reflect on how the piercing nature of Qoph can help you cut through these superficial layers to reveal the deeper truths beneath.

4. **Connect with the Divine:** As you focus on the image of Qoph, imagine it as a channel drawing down divine wisdom into your consciousness. Feel this wisdom as a soothing, enlightening presence in your mind, expanding your perceptions and deepening your understanding of the world and yourself.

5. **Set an Intention:** With each inhale, draw in clarity and insight; with each exhale, release confusion and prejudice. Set a personal intention to embrace the insights you gain, using them to guide your actions and decisions in a more informed and compassionate manner.

6. **Return to Presence:** Gradually bring your focus back to your physical surroundings. Wiggle your fingers and toes, stretch if needed, and when ready, open your eyes. Take a moment to reflect on your meditation and how you can apply the insights and intentions to your daily life.

CHAPTER 20

Resh: The Head of Renewal

Resh (ר)
Modern Hebrew Letter

Modern Resh ר is used in contemporary Hebrew.

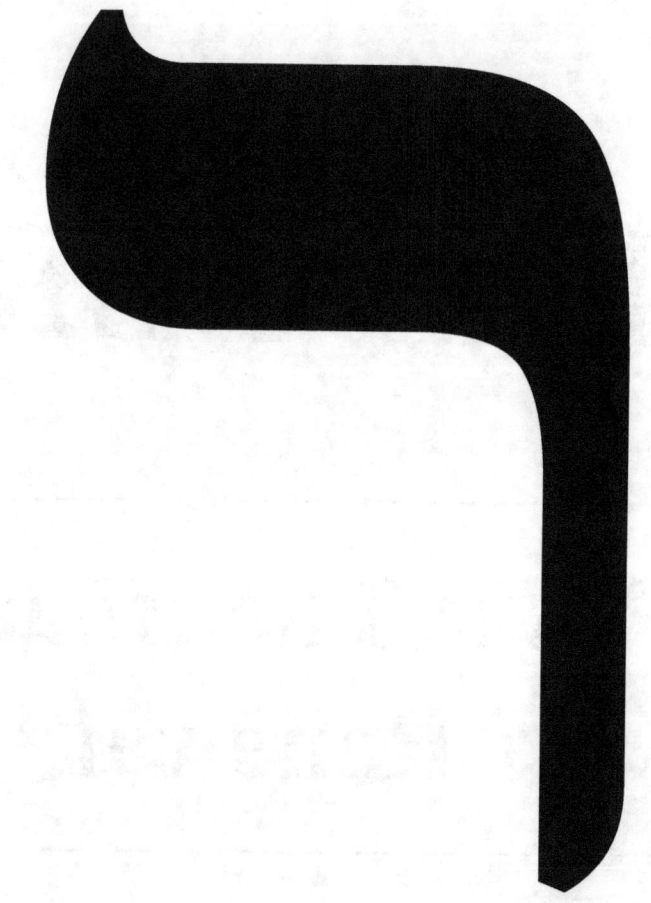

Ancient Pictorial/Glyph:(the head)

The ancient representation of Resh symbolizes the head, leader, and chief.

Introduction to Resh

Explore the twentieth letter of the Hebrew aleph-beth: Resh. This letter represents the head, a symbol of leadership, beginnings, and the renewal of purpose. It embodies the ideals of turning back to the right path and seeking new opportunities.

Name and Spellings

Resh, also spelled 'Reish,' represents the concept of the head, which stands for authority and direction. As you delve into Resh, reflect on its symbolic importance in renewal and leading with purpose.

Pronunciation Guide

Pronounced 'ray-sh,' similar to the 'r' in 'rain.' This sound rolls lightly off the tongue, emphasizing the smoothness and flexibility of Resh in guiding one's journey.

Corresponding Greek and English Letters

Resh corresponds to the Greek Rho (P, ρ) and the English letter R. All three share a strong consonantal presence, providing essential structure in their respective languages.

Numerical Value

In Hebrew numerology, Resh represents the number 200. This number symbolizes a turning point or change, reflecting the transformative potential of Resh in guiding renewal and new directions.

Resh as the Head of Renewal

Resh's form resembles a bowed head, symbolizing humility and readiness to receive wisdom. This form underscores Resh's function in signifying new beginnings, where renewal often comes from recognizing past mistakes and seeking better paths.

Spiritually, Resh embodies transformation and the willingness to turn back from wrong paths toward the light. It represents the head as the center of thought and purpose, guiding the entire body toward higher ideals. Resh is a reminder that no matter how far one strays, there is always an opportunity to return and realign with truth and goodness.

In mystical thought, Resh is associated with the concept of 'teshuvah,' or repentance, which invites reflection on past actions and a commitment to change. It serves as an inspiration to act with humility and align one's intentions with divine wisdom.

Resh is the Cosmic Mind. It is seen as a symbol of the human head but also as the Cosmic Mind, representing the universal consciousness that governs all of creation. This view extends Resh's symbolism beyond individual transformation to encompass the guiding intelligence that orders the cosmos. As such, Resh is often associated with the highest levels of spiritual enlightenment, where one's individual mind aligns with the universal mind, achieving profound insight and understanding of the nature of reality. This aspect of Resh emphasizes the interconnectedness of all things through the conduit of divine intellect.

Resh is a Social Leader. In addition to its spiritual implications, Resh is also symbolic of leadership and social responsibility. Just as the head directs the body, Resh symbolizes those who lead communities and make decisions that affect the collective. This letter encourages leaders to act with wisdom, foresight, and compassion, highlighting the need for ethical governance that reflects higher moral standards. In Hebrew, Resh begins words like "rosh" (head), "rav" (great, numerous), and "rishon" (first), which all convey aspects of leadership and primacy. This dimension of Resh serves as a reminder that true leadership is not about power but about guiding others toward greater good and collective advancement.

Interesting Fact

Resh is often associated with the divine attributes of mercy and compassion. It represents the idea that renewal requires acknowledging one's shortcomings and seeking to correct them with empathy and self-awareness.

In the study of sacred geometry within ancient teachings, the form of Resh is often analyzed for its unique shape that resembles a bending or bowing head. This shape is said to symbolize the moon at its crescent phase, representing renewal and cyclical change. It reflects the moon's role in marking time and its influence on the Earth. This connection suggests that Resh embodies personal transformation and repentance and also aligns with universal rhythms and cycles, emphasizing the natural flow of renewal of the cosmos.

Resh has a numerical value of 200, which, in mystical numerology, represents an amplified state of potentiality and transformation. The number 200 is considered powerful for its ability to signify great shifts and changes, echoing Resh's thematic focus on turning points and new beginnings. This number is often used in meditations and rituals that focus on overcoming past limitations and forging new paths. This aspect of Resh as a harbinger of significant change is particularly resonant in times of personal or communal upheaval, where the old ways are reconsidered and new directions are sought.

Spelling Resh (Resh, Aleph, Shin)

"The Head of Renewal (Resh) embodies Divine Unity (Aleph) and
Transformative Fire (Shin)."
The Hebrew spelling of Resh

ר א ש

Resh (ר): Symbolizes the head, representing beginnings, leadership, and the pursuit of knowledge. It also signifies humility and the readiness to receive wisdom.

Aleph (א): Represents divine unity, the source of all creation, and the connection between the physical and spiritual realms. It is the first letter of the Hebrew alphabet, symbolizing the oneness of God.

Shin (ש): Embodies transformative fire, purification, and divine energy. It represents change and the power to refine and elevate the spirit.

In this combination, Resh signifies a journey of renewal and transformation, guided by divine unity and the purifying fire of spiritual growth. It emphasizes the importance of beginnings, the pursuit of wisdom, and the continuous process of self-improvement and enlightenment.

Chapter Engagement: Resh Meditation

Meditating on Renewal and Guidance

1. **Prepare Your Space:** Find a quiet, comfortable place where you can sit undisturbed. Sit in a relaxed but upright position, close your eyes, and begin to focus on your breathing. Take deep, slow breaths to center yourself and calm your mind.

2. **Visualize Resh:** Imagine the letter Resh in your mind as a head that is bowed in humility yet poised to lead. Visualize this head radiating a gentle, illuminating light, representing wisdom and enlightenment.

3. **Contemplate Renewal:** Think about the aspects of your life that need renewal or transformation. Reflect on how the humility embodied by Resh can lead to new beginnings and greater wisdom. Consider how admitting past mistakes and learning from them can guide your future actions.

4. **Connect with Leadership:** As you focus on Resh, think about your role as a leader—whether in your family, community, or workplace. Consider how enlightened leadership, which combines wisdom and humility, can positively influence those around you.

5. **Set an Intention:** With each inhale, draw in clarity and insight; with each exhale, release stubbornness and pride. Set a personal intention to lead with wisdom and to embrace the process of renewal in your personal and professional life.

6. **Return to Presence:** Gradually bring your focus back to your physical surroundings. Wiggle your fingers and toes, stretch if needed, and when ready, open your eyes. Take a moment to reflect on your meditation and how you can apply the insights and intentions to your daily life.

CHAPTER 21

Shin: The Flame of Transformation

Shin (ש)
Modern Hebrew Letter

Modern Shin is used in contemporary Hebrew.

Ancient Pictorial/Glyph:(teeth or fire)

Ancient representation of Shin is symbolized by fire or teeth.

Introduction to Shin

Explore the twenty-first letter of the Hebrew aleph-beth: Shin. This letter symbolizes fire, transformation, and divine presence. It represents the dynamic power of change, renewal, and the everlasting flame of spiritual growth.

Name and Spellings

Shin, sometimes also spelled 'Sin,' embodies the concepts of both fire and teeth, reflecting the dual aspects of change and consumption. As you explore Shin, reflect on its role in bringing renewal through purposeful action.

Pronunciation Guide

Pronounced **'sheen'** or **'seen,'** depending on the position of the dot above the letter. With a dot on the right side, it's pronounced **'sheen,'** like **'sh'** in **'ship.'** With the dot on the left, it's **'seen,'** like **'s'** in **'sun.'** This dual pronunciation reflects Shin's versatility and adaptability.

Corresponding Greek and English Letters

Shin does not have a direct Greek equivalent but corresponds to the English letters S and SH. Its unique sound distinguishes it in forming a variety of words in Hebrew.

Numerical Value

In Hebrew numerology, Shin represents the number 300. This number is associated with transformation, fire, and the divine, mirroring Shin's role in spiritual growth and the pursuit of wisdom.

Shin as the Flame of Transformation

Shin's form resembles flames or teeth, embodying both the consuming and transformative nature of fire. It represents divine energy that both purifies and refines, bringing new life through the creative destruction of outdated patterns and perspectives.

Spiritually, Shin is considered the letter of divine presence, representing the Shekinah (the divine feminine presence) that dwells within all creation. It also symbolizes 'Shaddai,' one of Yahweh's names, highlighting its sacred role in embodying divine power.

The dual pronunciation of Shin, as **'sheen'** and **'seen,'** illustrates its dualistic nature. It invites us to embrace the ability to adapt and change based on life's circumstances, aligning our actions with the divine purpose. This adaptability allows Shin to be both creative and destructive, encouraging us to let go of what no longer serves us and create space for new growth.

Shin represents the flame of wisdom that burns within us, revealing truths and lighting the way toward spiritual fulfillment.

Shin's role extends beyond transformation to include the concept of protection and boundary-setting. Its resemblance to teeth is not only symbolic of consuming fire but also serves as a metaphor for the protective nature of teeth in the animal kingdom—defending, defining territory, and maintaining the integrity of the whole. In spiritual contexts, Shin is seen as a guardian of sacred spaces and spiritual truths. It embodies the protective aspect of Shaddai, a name of Yahweh often inscribed on mezuzahs (doorpost scroll cases) placed on the entrances of homes. This practice highlights Shin's role in safeguarding the dwellers by marking the boundaries that separate and sanctify the home space from the outer world.

In the broader cosmic scheme, Shin is associated with the element of fire, which is essential for balance within the classical elements (fire, water, air, earth). Shin's fiery nature represents the force of transformation that is necessary for the renewal of the cosmos. It is said to play a crucial role in the eschatological (end-times) visions within Kabbalistic traditions, where fire symbolizes both the end of old worlds and the purification necessary for the creation of new realities. This apocalyptic aspect of Shin underlines its importance in the cycles of destruction that precede creation, emphasizing the necessary clearing away of the old to make way for the new and purified world.

Interesting Fact

Shin is considered one of the letters inscribed on the mezuzah, a ritual object placed on the doorpost to signify divine protection over a household. It represents the unity and protection of the divine presence that surrounds us.

The letter Shin is intimately connected to the human anatomy, particularly the spine. The three branches of the Shin are said to symbolize the three main pillars of the human spinal column. This anatomical symbolism extends to spiritual interpretations, where the spine represents the central support structure that upholds spiritual vitality and strength. The Kabbalists believe that proper alignment of the spine during prayer and meditation enhances spiritual energy flow, mirroring the sacred structure of Shin and its role in channeling divine energy.

Shin's influence is also seen in sacred architecture, particularly in the design of some synagogues and study halls. The three branches of the Shin are often incorporated into the design of windows or archways, symbolizing the light of knowledge and wisdom entering the space. This architectural element is not just decorative but is intended to create a physical manifestation of Shin's spiritual qualities, fostering an environment conducive to learning and divine connection. This use of Shin in architectural elements underscores its role as a beacon of enlightenment and protector of sacred spaces.

Spelling of Shin (Shin, Yod, Nun)

"The Flame of Enlightenment (Shin) manifests (Yod) life and continuity (Nun)."

The Hebrew spelling of Shin is

שׁ י ן

Shin (שׁ): Represents the flame, symbolizing transformation, enlightenment, and divine presence.
Yod (י): Symbolizes manifestation, acting as a spark that brings ideas and divine energy into reality.
Nun (ן): Signifies life and continuity, emphasizing the enduring and evolving nature of the transformations initiated by Shin.

Together, these letters illustrate Shin's role in illuminating the spiritual path, bringing transformative insights into reality, and ensuring their continuation in life.

Chapter Engagement: Shin Meditation

Meditating on Transformation and Divine Presence

1. **Prepare Your Space:** Find a quiet, comfortable place where you can sit undisturbed. Sit in a relaxed but upright position, close your eyes, and begin to focus on your breathing. Take deep, slow breaths to center yourself and calm your mind.

2. **Visualize Shin:** Imagine the letter Shin in your mind as a bright, burning flame. Visualize this flame as vibrant and dynamic, constantly moving and transforming. See it radiating light and warmth, filling the space around you with its energy.

3. **Contemplate Transformation:** Think about the areas in your life that require transformation. Reflect on how the purifying fire of Shin can help burn away old patterns, beliefs, or behaviors that no longer serve you. Envision this transformative fire, preparing you for new beginnings and fresh perspectives.

4. **Connect with the Divine:** As you focus on the flame of Shin, consider its representation of the divine presence. Feel this presence as a guiding force in your life, illuminating your path and providing clarity. Allow yourself to feel supported and uplifted by this divine energy.

5. **Set an Intention:** With each inhale, draw in the transformative power of Shin; with each exhale, release resistance and fear. Set a personal intention to embrace change and seek deeper spiritual insights. Commit to using the energy of Shin to foster growth and renewal in your life.

6. **Return to Presence:** Gradually bring your focus back to your physical surroundings. Wiggle your fingers and toes, stretch if needed, and when ready, open your eyes. Take a moment to reflect on your meditation and how you can apply the insights and intentions to your daily life.

CHAPTER 22

Tav: The Mark of Truth

Tav (ת)

Modern Hebrew Letter

Modern Tav ת is used in contemporary Hebrew.

Ancient Pictorial/Glyph: (a cross, a mark)

The ancient representation of Tav symbolizes a cross or mark.

Introduction to Tav

Explore the twenty-second and final letter of the Hebrew aleph-beth: Tav. This letter represents a mark, sign, or cross, embodying the completion of a journey and the fulfillment of purpose. It serves as a testament to truth and divine connection.

Name and Spellings

Tav, sometimes also spelled 'Tau' and 'Taw,' represents the concept of a sign or mark. As you explore Tav, consider its significance as a symbol that seals or completes a cycle.

Pronunciation Guide

Pronounced 'tahv,' similar to the 't' in 'table.' The sound is crisp and firm, representing Tav's finality and certainty in bringing completion.

Corresponding Greek and English Letters

Tav corresponds to the Greek Tau (T, τ) and the English letter T. These counterparts share Tav's strong consonantal presence, emphasizing its role in marking the end of words and ideas.

Numerical Value

In Hebrew numerology, Tav represents the number 400. This number is associated with fulfillment, completion, and wholeness, reflecting Tav's role in closing the cycle of the Hebrew alphabet.

Tav as the Mark of Truth

Tav's form resembles a cross or a mark, indicating completion or a seal. This form emphasizes Tav's role as the final letter, marking the culmination of a journey or a process and symbolizing a commitment to truth.

Spiritually, Tav represents truth and perfection. In Kabbalistic thought, Tav is associated with the concept of **'emet'** (truth), where the mark signifies the complete integration of divine wisdom. It challenges us to embody truth in our words and actions, aligning ourselves with the divine will.

Tav also marks the covenant between humanity and Yahweh, symbolizing a divine promise that has been fulfilled. Its form signifies an alignment with purpose and a commitment to integrity in the journey of life. This alignment requires careful reflection on one's path to ensure that the destination honors the divine truth within.

Tav is the Symbol of Cosmic Completion. Beyond individual spiritual journeys, it is also cosmic and the ultimate realization of the universe's purpose. In esoteric teachings, Tav is considered the last letter not just in the sequence of the alphabet but also in the grand cosmic cycle, marking the **'end'** that inevitably leads to a new 'beginning.' This cyclical concept reflects the belief in ongoing creation and destruction, a fundamental principle in many spiritual traditions. Tav symbolizes the moment of transcendence where all dualities are unified, and the spiritual merges with the material, leading to a new phase of existence. This overarching closure and renewal offer a broader, universal perspective on Tav's role in the spiritual evolution of all beings.

Tav is the Guardian of Law and Order. Tav was often used as an actual mark or signature on documents, denoting completion, authenticity, and agreement. This historical use underpins its spiritual significance as a guardian of divine law and order. Just as it was used to validate and finalize earthly agreements, spiritually, Tav is seen as affirming the divine laws that govern the universe. It emphasizes the importance of adhering to these spiritual laws, serving as a reminder of the divine order that underlies all of creation. This aspect of Tav stresses the accountability and responsibility of living in accordance with cosmic laws, promoting a life lived with integrity and in harmony with the divine plan.

Interesting Fact

Tav is considered a symbol of the redemption and renewal that comes from spiritual growth. Its presence marks the completion of the sacred alphabet, illustrating the journey from creation to perfection, from Aleph to Tav.

In ancient Semitic inscriptions, the symbol for Tav was often used to signify ownership or a mark of craftsmanship. This practice extends Tav's symbolic meaning from merely a letter in the alphabet to a mark of authenticity and authority in historical contexts. Archaeologists have interpreted artifacts bearing the Tav symbol as items that were marked to indicate possession or to confer a blessing. This historical usage underscores Tav's role as a protective and authoritative symbol, signifying not just the end of an item's creation but also its readiness for sacred or everyday use.

In mystical Jewish texts, Tav is considered particularly potent when discussing the concept of sealing divine attributes. For instance, in the Zohar, the book of mystical Jewish thought, Tav is described as the seal of truth, the final seal on the High Priest's garments, symbolizing the completion and perfection of divine service. This representation of Tav as a seal extends to the esoteric belief that Tav seals the six directions of the world (north, south, east, west, up, down) in the divine name, maintaining balance and order in the universe. This connection illustrates how Tav is considered fundamental in maintaining cosmic stability and integrity, bridging spiritual principles with the physical realm.

Spelling Tav (Tav, Yod, Wav)

"The Mark of Truth (Tav) is established by Divine Guidance (Yod)
and Connection (Wav)."

The Hebrew spelling of Tav

ת י ו

Tav (ת): Represents a mark or sign, symbolizing completion, truth, and the fulfillment of purpose. It is the last letter of the Hebrew alphabet, indicating the end of a journey or process.

Yod (י): Symbolizes divine guidance, a point of light, creativity, and spiritual insight. It connects the material world with the divine, highlighting the influence of higher wisdom in our actions.

Wav (ו): Represents connection, a hook, or a link, emphasizing unity and continuity. It connects heaven and earth, illustrating the bond between the spiritual and physical realms.

In this combination, Tav embodies the culmination of a spiritual journey marked by truth and divine fulfillment. It signifies the role of divine guidance and connection in achieving ultimate truth and completeness, highlighting the integration of spiritual insights and the unity of all creation.

Chapter Engagement: Tav Meditation

Meditating on Truth and Completion

1. **Prepare Your Space:** Find a quiet, comfortable place where you can sit undisturbed. Sit in a relaxed but upright position, close your eyes, and begin to focus on your breathing. Take deep, slow breaths to center yourself and calm your mind.

2. **Visualize Tav:** Imagine the letter Tav in your mind as a strong, solid mark or seal. Visualize it as the completion of a circle, the final piece that completes and perfects a complex design. See it radiating a sense of wholeness and integrity, symbolizing the fulfillment of a divine promise or plan.

3. **Contemplate Truth:** Reflect on the concept of truth in your life. Think about areas where you seek greater honesty and integrity. Consider how embodying the truth of Tav can influence your decisions and interactions. Meditate on the idea of Tav as the seal of truth on your actions and thoughts, committing you to live authentically.

4. **Connect with Divine Purpose:** As you focus on the symbol of Tav, think about your own life's completion and fulfillment. Contemplate your goals and aspirations and how you can align them more closely with your true purpose. Feel Tav's energy helping you to seal these intentions, turning them into commitments.

5. **Set an Intention:** With each inhale, draw in clarity and purpose; with each exhale, release confusion and uncertainty. Set a personal intention to embrace the qualities of Tav in your life—truth, completeness, and integrity. Decide on one practical way you can demonstrate these qualities in your daily actions.

6. **Return to Presence:** Gradually bring your focus back to your physical surroundings. Wiggle your fingers and toes, stretch if needed, and when ready, open your eyes. Take a moment to reflect on your meditation and how you can apply the insights and intentions to your daily life.

CONCLUSION

Embracing the Divine Language of Aleph-Beth

As we conclude our journey through the Hebrew Aleph-Beth, we find ourselves not merely at the end of a study but at the threshold of a deeper spiritual awakening. The letters of the Aleph-Beth are far more than symbols for sounds; they are powerful vessels of divine energy, each carrying unique vibrations and secrets that connect us directly to Yahweh and the fabric of creation.

The Mystical Power of the Aleph-Beth

Throughout this book, we've explored how each letter serves as a conduit for divine wisdom and spiritual illumination. From Aleph, representing oneness and the divine breath of creation, to Tav, the mark of truth and completion, every letter embodies profound metaphysical and spiritual principles. The Aleph-Beth is a sacred alphabet that forms the very building blocks of the universe, bridging the gap between the seen and unseen, the material and the spiritual.

Connection to Yahweh

Studying the Aleph-Beth has opened a gateway to experiencing a closer relationship with Yahweh. Each letter offers a unique aspect of the divine, inviting us to integrate these spiritual truths into our daily lives. This alignment with Yahweh transforms us, nurturing our souls and guiding our actions toward higher purposes. The letters teach us to see beyond the ordinary, to perceive the divine hand in every aspect of existence, and to understand our place within this sacred tapestry.

Aligning with Your Spirit

As you have journeyed through the Aleph-Beth, you have also embarked on a path of self-discovery. The Hebrew letters encourage introspection and spiritual growth, helping you to align more closely with your own spirit. This alignment brings clarity, peace, and a profound sense of purpose. By meditating on and internalizing the lessons of each letter, you strengthen your connection to your true self and the divine essence within you.

Hidden Wisdom and Continuing Revelation

The study of the Aleph-Beth is not a finite journey but an ongoing revelation. Each letter is a gateway to infinite wisdom and spiritual insight. As you continue to reflect on these letters, new layers of meaning and hidden truths will unfold. The Hebrew alphabet is a living, breathing entity, constantly revealing new dimensions of the divine to those who seek with a pure heart and open mind.

A Call to Continued Exploration

We hope this book has ignited a passion for the Aleph-Beth within you. The letters are keys to unlocking the mysteries of the universe, tools for spiritual growth, and bridges to a deeper connection with Yahweh. As you continue your studies, may you find joy in discovering the limitless potential and divine power encoded within each letter. Let this be the beginning of a lifelong journey of learning, reflection, and spiritual awakening.

Embrace the Aleph-Beth

In embracing the Aleph-Beth, you are embracing a sacred tradition that has the power to transform your life. These letters are not just ancient symbols; they are divine gifts that guide you toward a more profound understanding of the universe and your place within it. As you move forward, carry the wisdom of the Aleph-Beth with you, allowing it to illuminate your path, enrich your spirit, and deepen your connection with Yahweh.

May your journey with the Aleph-Beth continue to inspire, uplift, and transform you. The divine language of Yahweh is now a part of you, a source of endless wisdom and spiritual nourishment. Embrace it, cherish it, and let it guide you to new heights of spiritual understanding and oneness with the Creator.

GLOSSARY TERMS

7 Oaths: The 7 Oaths are references to significant biblical oaths or covenants, often linked to divine promises or commands. These oaths are seen as solemn agreements between God and humanity, carrying profound spiritual and moral obligations. They represent key moments of divine commitment and human responsibility in the biblical narrative.

7 Seals: The 7 Seals, as described in the biblical context, specifically in the Book of Revelation, are emblematic seals that signify events occurring during the end times. Each seal, when broken, unleashes a specific event or series of events that lead to the ultimate fulfillment of divine prophecy. These seals are central to the apocalyptic vision and the unfolding of God's final plan for humanity.

Abba: Biblical title of honor, literally "father," used as an invocation of God Yahweh, from Latin abba, from Greek abba, from Aramaic (Semitic) abba, "the father, my father." From the emphatic state of abh, "father" is often used to express intimacy with God.

Alexandria: An ancient city in Egypt, a center of Hellenistic culture and scholarship. A city in Egypt, founded 332 B.C.E. by Alexander the Great, for whom it is named.

Angels: An angel is "one of a class of spiritual beings, attendants and messengers of God," a c. 1300 fusion of Old English engel (with hard -g-) and Old French angele—also a Divine Messenger.

Apt: Suitable or appropriate in the circumstances. The word "apt" comes from the Latin "aptus," meaning "fit" or "suitable." It describes something that is especially appropriate or fitting for a particular situation or purpose.

Aramaic: A Semitic language closely related to Hebrew, used widely in the ancient Near East. The name "Aramaic" derives from "Aram," the ancient region and people of central Syria. Aramaic became the lingua franca of the Near East from the 6th century BCE onward due to its adoption by the Persian Empire for administrative purposes.

Axis Mundi: A concept representing the connection between Heaven and Earth, the world's center. The term "axis mundi" is Latin for "axis of the world." It is a symbolic concept in various religions and mythologies, representing the world's center where the earthly and divine realms intersect.

Babylonia: An ancient Akkadian-speaking state and cultural region based in central-southern Mesopotamia. The name "Babylonia" comes from the city of Babylon, which means "Gate of the Gods" (Akkadian: "Bāb-ili"). Babylonia was a major political and cultural center in ancient Mesopotamia.

Canaanite: Refers to the ancient people and cultures of the land of Canaan. The term "Canaanite" originates from "Canaan," the name of a region that encompassed parts of modern-day Israel, Palestine, Lebanon, and Syria. The Canaanites were known for their trade and cultural interactions with neighboring civilizations.

Chaldean: This refers to ancient Semitic-speaking people who lived in Chaldea, a region located in southern Babylonia. The term "Chaldean" comes from "Kaldu," the Akkadian name for the Chaldean people. They are known for their contributions to astronomy and astrology and for their role in the Neo-Babylonian Empire.

Consonants: Speech sounds produced with some closure of the vocal tract. The word "consonant" comes from the Latin "consonare," meaning "to sound together," highlighting that consonants are often sounded together with vowels in speech.

Corresponding: Having a close similarity or connection. The word "corresponding" derives from the Latin "correspondere," from "com-" (together) and "respondere" (to answer). It implies a mutual relationship or connection between two or more things.

Cosmic: Pertaining to the universe or cosmos, especially in an orderly and harmonious system. The word "cosmic" originates from the Greek "kosmikos," which means "relating to the cosmos" or "orderly."

Creator: One who brings something into existence, often referring to God. The term "creator" comes from the Latin "creator," derived from "creare," meaning "to create."

Creation: The act of bringing something into existence, often referring to the universe created by God. The word "creation" stems from the Latin "creatio," from "creare," meaning "to create."

Daniel: A prophet in the Hebrew Bible, known for his wisdom and revelations. The name "Daniel" comes from the Hebrew "Daniyyel," meaning "God is my judge."

Dialectics: The art of investigating or discussing the truth of opinions. The term "dialectics" comes from the Greek "dialektikē," meaning "the art of discourse."

Dichotomy: A division or contrast between two things that are represented as being entirely different. The word "dichotomy" comes from the Greek "dichotomia," from "dicha" (in two) and "temnein" (to cut).

Divine Essence: The intrinsic nature or indispensable quality of God. "Divine" comes from the Latin "divinus," meaning "of a god," and "essence" from the Latin "essentia," meaning "being" or "substance."

Divine Presence: The presence of God in the world and within the believers. "Divine" comes from the Latin "divinus," meaning "of a god," and "presence" from the Latin "praesentia," meaning "being at hand."

Dwelling: A place where one lives, often referring to a spiritual or holy place. The word "dwelling" originates from the Old English "dwellan," meaning "to lead astray" or "to remain."

Dual: Consisting of two parts or elements. The term "dual" comes from the Latin "dualis," from "duo," meaning "two."

Duality: The quality or condition of being dual, often representing opposites like good and evil. The word "duality" derives from the Latin "dualis," meaning "containing two."

Egypt: A country in North Africa with a rich ancient history. The name "Egypt" comes from the Greek "Aigyptos," derived from the ancient Egyptian name "Hwt-Ka-Ptah," meaning "House of the Ka (soul) of Ptah" (an important deity in ancient Egypt).

Enclosure: An area that is sealed off with an artificial or natural barrier. The word "enclosure" comes from the Old French "enclos," meaning "closed in."

English: A West Germanic language that is the primary language of several countries, including the United States and the United Kingdom. The name "English" comes from "Englisc," the Old English term for the language of the Angles, one of the Germanic tribes that settled in England.

Essence: The intrinsic nature or indispensable quality of something that determines its character. The word "essence" originates from the Latin "essentia," derived from "esse," meaning "to be."

Exhalations: The process of breathing out air from the lungs; in a spiritual or metaphorical context, it can refer to the release of energy, breath, or spirit. The word "exhalation" comes from the Latin "exhalare," meaning "to breathe out."

Existence: The fact or state of living or having objective reality. The word "existence" comes from the Latin "existere," meaning "to stand out" or "to emerge."

Ezra: A Hebrew scribe and leader who returned from Babylonian exile and helped reestablish Hebrew law and practice. The name "Ezra" derives from the Hebrew "Ezra," meaning "help" or "helper." Known for his critical role in compiling and editing the Torah, Ezra's efforts were foundational in restoring Jewish religious and social life after the exile.

Foundation: The basis or groundwork of anything. The term "foundation" comes from the Latin "fundatio," derived from "fundare," meaning "to lay a base for." It denotes the underlying support or starting point for a structure, system, or set of principles.

Gezer Calendar: An ancient inscription from Israel listing agricultural activities, one of the earliest examples of Hebrew writing. Discovered in the ancient city of Gezer, this calendar dates back to the 10th century BCE and provides valuable insights into the agricultural practices and early writing systems of the Israelites.

Gematria: An Ancient Israelite form of numerology where letters have numerical values. The word "gematria" originates from the Greek "geometria," which means "geometry," reflecting the ancient practice of assigning numerical values to letters to find hidden meanings in words and texts.

Glyph: A symbolic figure or character usually carved or inscribed. The term "glyph" comes from the Greek "glyphē," meaning "carving." Glyphs are used in various writing systems and art forms to convey specific meanings or functions.

Greek: Relating to Greece, its people, or their language. The word "Greek" originates from the Latin "Graecus," which in turn comes from the Greek "Graikoi," the name of a Greek tribe. Greece has a rich cultural and historical heritage, influential in philosophy, art, and science.

Hebrew: The ancient language of the Israelites, in which the Hebrew Bible is written. The term "Hebrew" comes from the Latin "Hebraeus," which derives from the Greek "Hebraios," and ultimately from the Hebrew "Eber, Ivri," meaning "one from the other side."

Hebrew Bible: The Hebrew Bible is the canonical collection of Hebrew texts (Genesis to Malachi), which is known as the Christian Old Testament. Known as the Tanakh in Judaism, it includes the Torah (Law), Nevi'im (Prophets), and Ketuvim (Writings).

Hellenistic Jew: Jews who adopted the Greek language and culture during and after the conquests of Alexander the Great. The term "Hellenistic" comes from the Greek "Hellēn," meaning "Greek." These Jews often blended Greek and Hebrew Israelite traditions in their practices and writings.

Humility: A modest or low view of one's importance; humbleness. The word "humility" comes from the Latin "humilitas," from "humilis," meaning "low" or "grounded." It is often valued as a virtue in many religious and philosophical traditions.

Illuminations: The process of lighting up or the state of being illuminated, often used metaphorically for spiritual enlightenment. The term "illumination" derives from the Latin "illuminatio," from "illuminare," meaning "to light up."

Inhalation: The act of breathing in. The word "inhalation" comes from the Latin "inhalare," from "in-" (into) and "halare" (to breathe). It refers to the intake of air into the lungs.

Introspection: The examination of one's own thoughts and feelings. The term "introspection" comes from the Latin "introspicere," meaning "to look inside." It is a reflective practice aimed at self-awareness and understanding.

Israel: A country in the Middle East, historically the homeland of the Israelites and now Jewish people. The name "Israel" comes from the Hebrew "Yisrael," meaning "he who struggles with God," a name given to the patriarch Jacob (Yaacob).

Israelites: Members of the ancient Hebrew nation, especially in the period from the Exodus to the Babylonian Captivity. The term "Israelite" derives from "Israel," the name given to Jacob (Yaacob) and his descendants.

Judah: An ancient kingdom of the Southern Levant, the land of the tribe of Judah. The name "Judah" comes from the Hebrew "Yehuwdah," meaning "praise, prayer, and worship." Judah is the fourth of the twelve tribes of Israel and later became a significant kingdom.

Kabbalah: A form of Jewish mysticism that seeks to understand the nature of God and the universe. The term "Kabbalah" comes from the Hebrew "qabbalah," meaning "reception" or "tradition." It involves esoteric teachings about the divine, creation, and the nature of the soul.

Linga Franca: A language that is adopted as a common language between speakers whose native languages are different. The term "lingua franca" originates from Italian, meaning "Frankish tongue," and was historically used to describe a trade language in the Mediterranean. It facilitates communication and trade among people with different native languages.

Light: Often symbolizes divine presence, truth, and spiritual illumination. The word "light" comes from the Old English "leoht," derived from the Proto-Germanic "leuhtam." Light is a powerful metaphor in many spiritual traditions, representing enlightenment and the presence of the divine.

Linguistic: Relating to language or linguistics. The term "linguistic" comes from the Latin "linguisticus," derived from "lingua," meaning "tongue" or "language." It pertains to the scientific study of language and its structure.

Masorites: Jewish scribes who created the vowel point system to preserve the pronunciation of the Hebrew Bible. The name "Masorites" comes from the Hebrew "Masorah," meaning "tradition." Their work, done between the 6th and 10th centuries CE, ensured the accurate transmission of the biblical text.

Meditation: A practice where an individual uses a technique to focus the mind on a particular object, thought, or activity to achieve a mentally clear and emotionally calm state. The word "meditation" originates from the Latin "meditatio," from "meditari," meaning "to think, contemplate, devise, ponder." It is a central practice in many spiritual traditions.

Metaphysics: Metaphysics is a branch of philosophy that explores the nature of being, existence, and reality. The term "metaphysics" comes from the Greek "meta" (beyond) and "physika" (physics), referring to the study of what lies beyond the physical world.

Mundane: Lacking interest or excitement; dull; also refers to the earthly world as opposed to the spiritual. The word "mundane" comes from the Latin "mundanus," derived from "mundus," meaning "world." It often contrasts the ordinary with the extraordinary or spiritual.

Mystical: Relating to mysticism or religious mystic practices involving direct communication with the divine or spiritual truth. The term "mystical" comes from the Greek "mystikos," meaning "secret" or "mysterious." It involves seeking a direct personal experience of the divine.

Nehemiah: An Israelite leader who supervised the rebuilding of Jerusalem in the 5th century BCE after the Babylonian exile. The name "Nehemiah" comes from the Hebrew "Nechemya," meaning "comforted by Yahweh." His leadership is documented in the biblical Book of Nehemiah.

Nourishment: The food or other substances necessary for growth, health, and good condition. The word "nourishment" comes from the Old French word "nourishment," which is derived from "nourrir," meaning "to feed." It encompasses both physical and metaphorical sustenance.

Oneness: The state of being unified or whole, especially in the context of spiritual unity with God. The term "oneness" comes from the Old English "an," meaning "one." It denotes a state of harmony and unity with Yahweh, the divine, or the universe.

Paleo-Hebrew: An ancient script used to write Hebrew before the adoption of the square script. The term "Paleo-Hebrew" refers to the script used in inscriptions from the first millennium BCE, resembling the Phoenician alphabet.

Persian: Relating to Persia (modern-day Iran) or its people. The word "Persian" comes from "Persia," the Greek name for Iran, which itself is derived from "Pars," a region of southern Iran. Persia was known for its rich cultural heritage and significant historical empires.

Phoenician: An ancient Semitic-speaking civilization that spread across the Mediterranean; their alphabet was the precursor to many modern scripts. The name "Phoenician" comes from the Greek "Phoinix," referring to the region of modern-day Lebanon. Their maritime trade and alphabet significantly influenced other cultures.

Reconciliation: The restoration of friendly relations, making one view or belief compatible with another. The term "reconciliation" comes from the Latin "reconciliatio," from "reconciliare," meaning "to bring together again." It involves resolving differences and restoring harmony.

Repentance: The action of repenting; sincere regret or remorse. The word "repentance" comes from the Old French "repentir," meaning "to feel regret." It involves a recognition of wrongdoing and a commitment to change one's behavior.

Resonant: Deep, clear, and continuing to sound or ring; having the ability to evoke enduring emotions or responses. The term "resonant" comes from the Latin "resonare," meaning "to sound again." It describes sounds that linger and impact the listener emotionally or spiritually.

Rome: The capital city of Italy, historically significant as the center of the Roman Empire, is one of the most powerful civilizations in ancient history, and it profoundly influenced law, governance, architecture, and language. The name "Rome" comes from the Latin "Roma," with its exact etymology uncertain. The city's legacy continues to shape Western culture and society.

Root word: The base form of a word from which other words are derived. The term "root word" is used in linguistics to refer to the fundamental part of a word, providing its primary meaning. It is the foundation from which prefixes and suffixes can be added to form new words.

Sanctuary: A place of refuge or safety, often referring to a sacred place. The term "sanctuary" comes from the Latin "sanctuarium," from "sanctus," meaning "holy." It denotes a sacred or protected space where individuals seek solace, safety, or spiritual connection.

Sabbath: A day of religious observance and abstinence from work, kept by Jews from Friday evening to Saturday evening and by most Christians on Sunday. The word "Sabbath" comes from the Hebrew "Shabbat," meaning "rest" or "cessation." It is a day dedicated to rest and worship, commemorating God's rest after the creation.

Separation: The action or state of moving or being moved apart. The word "separation" comes from the Latin "separatio," from "separare," meaning "to divide" or "to part." It refers to the process or state of being set apart or divided from something else.

Sofit forms: The special final forms of certain Hebrew letters that appear at the end of words. The term "sofit" is derived from the Hebrew "sof," meaning "end." These forms are used in Hebrew writing to indicate that a letter is at the end of a word, altering its appearance.

Spiritual: Relating to or affecting the human spirit or soul as opposed to material or physical things. The word "spiritual" comes from the Latin "spiritualis," from "spiritus," meaning "breath" or "soul." It refers to matters concerning the non-material aspects of life, such as faith, values, and consciousness.

Spiritual illumination: Enlightenment or insight into spiritual truths. The term "illumination" comes from the Latin "illuminatio," from "illuminare," meaning "to light up." It describes the process of gaining profound spiritual understanding and clarity.

Spiritual temple: A sacred place dedicated to spiritual practices and divine presence. The term "temple" comes from the Latin "templum," meaning "a consecrated place." A spiritual temple is where individuals engage in worship, meditation, and other practices to connect with the divine.

Study: The devotion of time and attention to acquiring knowledge on an academic subject. The word "study" comes from the Latin "studium," meaning "zeal" or "pursuit." It involves focused effort to learn and understand various topics.

Symbolism: The use of symbols to represent ideas or qualities. The term "symbolism" comes from the Greek "symbolon," meaning "token" or "sign." It is a literary and artistic device where symbols are used to convey deeper meanings and concepts.

Tetragrammaton: The Greek word for the four Hebrew letters יהוה, the biblical name of God, YHWH (Yahweh). The term "tetragrammaton" comes from the Greek words "tetra" (four) and "gramma" (letter). It represents the four-letter name referring to the sacred and ineffable name of YHWH (Yahweh), replaced by the word "LORD" in Hebrew scripture.

Threshold: The point of entry or beginning; a boundary. The word "threshold" comes from the Old English "therscold," meaning "doorway" or "entrance." It symbolizes a point of transition from one state or condition to another.

Torah: The central reference of the religious Judaic tradition, often referring to the first five books of the Hebrew Bible. The term "Torah" comes from the Hebrew root "yarah," meaning "to teach" or "instruction." It encompasses the laws, teachings, and history fundamental to the Hebrew faith.

Transcendence: Existence or experience beyond the normal or physical level. The word "transcendence" comes from the Latin "transcendere," meaning "to climb over" or "to surpass." It refers to going beyond ordinary limits to reach a higher state of being or understanding.

Traverses: Travels across or through. The term "traverses" comes from the Latin "traversare," from "trans-" (across) and "vertere" (to turn). It means to move or pass through an area or space.

Wax and Wane: Increase and decrease, as in phases of the moon, or intensity or extent. The phrase "wax and wane" comes from the Old English "weaxan" (to grow) and "wanian" (to diminish). It describes cyclical growth and decline.

Yahweh: The Hebrew name for God in the Hebrew Bible. The name "Yahweh" is derived from the Tetragrammaton, YHWH, which represents God's divine name revealed to Moses in the book of Exodus. It is considered the most sacred name of God in Judaism.

Zerubbabel: A Hebrew leader who led the first group of Israelites who returned from the Babylonian Captivity and rebuilt the Temple in Jerusalem. The name "Zerubbabel" comes from the Hebrew "Zerubavel," meaning "seed of Babylon." He played a significant role in the restoration of Jewish worship and community life after the exile.

Zohar: A foundational work in the literature of mystical thought known as Kabbalah. The term "Zohar" comes from the Hebrew word for "splendor" or "radiance." Traditionally attributed to Rabbi Shimon bar Yochai, it was written in the late 13th century by Moses de León and explores mystical interpretations of the Torah.

References and Resources

"The Zohar" by Daniel C. Matt
The modern translation and commentary on one of the central works of Kabbalistic literature.

"Sefer Yetzirah: The Book of Creation" by Aryeh Kaplan
An authoritative translation and commentary on this foundational Kabbalistic text.

"The Power of the Aleph-Bet: Teachings from the Kabbalah" by Yitzchak Ginsburgh
A comprehensive study on the mystical significance of the Hebrew letters.

"Wisdom in the Hebrew Alphabet" by Michael L. Munk
An exploration of the spiritual and symbolic meanings of the Hebrew letters.

"Kabbalah: A Very Short Introduction" by Joseph Dan
A concise and accessible introduction to the history and principles of Kabbalah.

"The Book of Letters: A Mystical Hebrew Alphabet" by Lawrence Kushner
A popular work that explores the spiritual insights and meditations associated with each Hebrew letter.

"The Complete Art Scroll Siddur" by Nosson Scherman
An English translation and commentary on the traditional Jewish prayer book, with insights into the use of Hebrew.

"The Essential Kabbalah: The Heart of Jewish Mysticism" by Daniel C. Matt
An anthology of essential Kabbalistic texts translated and annotated.

"Etymological Dictionary of Biblical Hebrew" by Matityahu Clark
A comprehensive reference work that explores the roots and meanings of Hebrew words.

"The Oxford Dictionary of English Etymology" by C. T. Onions
A detailed etymological dictionary for English words, helpful for comparative studies with Hebrew.

"The Concise Oxford Dictionary of Linguistics" by P.H. Matthews
An essential reference for terms and concepts in linguistics.

"The Hidden Meaning of Dreams" by Craig Hamilton-Parker
A guide to interpreting the metaphysical and symbolic meanings of dreams.

"God is a Verb: Kabbalah and the Practice of Mystical Judaism" by David A. Cooper
A practical guide to incorporating Kabbalistic principles into everyday life.

"The Thirteen Petalled Rose: A Discourse on the Essence of Jewish Existence and Belief" by Adin Steinsaltz
It is an insightful work on the spiritual principles underlying Jewish belief and practice.

"Hebrew Myths: The Book of Genesis" by Robert Graves and Raphael Patai
A retelling and analysis of the myths and stories in the Book of Genesis.

"The New Strong's Exhaustive Concordance of the Bible" by James Strong
A comprehensive concordance for studying biblical texts with Hebrew and Greek dictionaries.

"Meditation and Kabbalah" by Aryeh Kaplan
An exploration of the meditative practices within the Kabbalistic tradition.

"The Kabbalah Handbook: A Concise Encyclopedia of Terms and Concepts in Jewish Mysticism" by Gabriella Samuel
An encyclopedia that provides clear and concise definitions and explanations of key terms and concepts in Kabbalah.

"Mystical Qabalah" by Dion Fortune
It is a classic work that explores the mystical aspects of the Qabalah, providing insights into its use and significance.

"The Kabbalistic Tradition: An Anthology of Jewish Mysticism," edited by Alan Unterman
An anthology of texts from the Kabbalistic tradition, offering insights into Jewish mystical thought.

"The Essential Zohar: The Source of Kabbalistic Wisdom" by Rav P.S. Berg
A guide to the Zohar, making its teachings accessible to a contemporary audience.

"The Alef-Beit: Jewish Thought Revealed through the Hebrew Letters" by Yitzchak Ginsburgh
An exploration of the spiritual and mystical meanings of the Hebrew alphabet.

"The Bahir: The Early Kabbalistic Text," translated by Aryeh Kaplan
A translation and commentary on the Sefer HaBahir, one of the earliest Kabbalistic texts.

"A Guide to the Zohar" by Arthur Green
An introduction and guide to understanding the Zohar and its place in Jewish mysticism.

"The Hebrew Letters: Channels of Creative Consciousness" by Rabbi Michael L. Munk
A study of the Hebrew letters as spiritual symbols and their role in Jewish thought and practice.

"Understanding Jewish Mysticism: A Source Reader," edited by David R. Blumenthal
A source reader that provides primary texts from Jewish mystical literature, with commentary and analysis.

"Etymological Dictionary of the Hebrew Language" by Ernest Klein
A comprehensive etymological dictionary that explores the roots and meanings of Hebrew words.

"The Qabalah of 50 Gates" by Steven Ashe
An exploration of the 50 Gates of Understanding, a key concept in Kabbalistic thought.

"The Hidden Treasures of Ancient Qabalah" by Elias Gewurz
A study of the hidden meanings and teachings within the Qabalah, focusing on its spiritual applications.

"A Kabbalistic Universe" by Z'ev ben Shimon Halevi
An introduction to Kabbalistic cosmology and its implications for understanding the universe and human existence.

"The Jewish Alchemists: A History and Source Book" by Raphael Patai
A study of the role of Jewish mystics in the history of alchemy, providing historical context and primary sources.

"Kabbalah and Exodus" by Z'ev ben Shimon Halevi
A study of the mystical interpretation of the Exodus narrative through the lens of Kabbalah.

"The Healing Power of Hebrew Letters" by Rabbi Yitzchak Ginsburgh
An exploration of the healing properties attributed to the Hebrew letters within Jewish mystical thought.

ABOUT THE AUTHOR

The Kingdom of Shalom - Truth, Holiness, Love, and Righteousness is a global spiritual organization created to honor and glorify God Yahweh. Our mission is to spread Yahweh's wisdom worldwide, illuminating hearts and minds to create a world of peace and prosperity.

As a global spiritual center, our theme is "Peace on Earth and Good Will for all minds in the world." Driven by a single goal, we aim to share Yahweh's Spirit, which embodies the wisdom, knowledge, and understanding necessary to bring forth "Minds of Peace."

We are the premier Israelite Center of Yahweh, restoring people to a covenant relationship with Him and leading them back to His true, holy, and righteous knowledge. Anchored in timeless wisdom and the values of Melchizedek, New Yerushalayim (Jerusalem), and Tziyon (Zion), our teachings illuminate readers with spiritual knowledge.

We offer transformative messages of spiritual illumination that create **"New Minds"** capable of engaging in **"Good Works."** These **"New Minds"** positively impact their own lives and those around them, spreading goodwill to foster a better world.

As a global spiritual educational center, we promote the divine wisdom of Yahweh through our books, lessons, programs, and products. This wisdom fosters completeness, safety, and soundness in body and mind. Our teachings bring health, happiness, and prosperity through righteous behavior and alignment with Yahweh, promoting introspection, harmony, and renewed purpose.

Join us on this spiritual journey to discover the transformative power of Yahweh's knowledge. Together, let us fill the earth with His Spirit, creating a world of peace, harmony, and goodwill.

The Kingdom of Shalom, the Kingdom of Peace, The Kingdom of Melchizedek, New Yerushalayim (Jerusalem), and Tziyon (Zion).

"You will know me by my works."
~James 2:18KJV

Bibliography

Berg, Philip S. The Essential Zohar: *The Source of Kabbalistic Wisdom. Bell Tower, 2002.*

Cooper, David A. God is a Verb: *Kabbalah and the Practice of Mystical Judaism. Riverhead Books, 1998.*

Dan, Joseph. Kabbalah: *A Very Short Introduction. Oxford University Press, 2007.*

Dennis, Geoffrey W. *The Encyclopedia of Jewish Myth, Magic and Mysticism. Llewellyn Publications, 2007.*

Fortune, Dion. *Mystical Qabalah. Weiser Books, 2000.*

Ginsburgh, Yitzchak. *The Alef-Beit: Jewish Thought Revealed through the Hebrew Letters. Jason Aronson, 1995.*

Ginsburgh, Yitzchak. *The Power of the Aleph-Bet: Teachings from the Kabbalah. Gal Einai, 1990.*

Green, Arthur. *A Guide to the Zohar. Stanford University Press, 2004.*

Kaplan, Aryeh. *Meditation and Kabbalah. Samuel Weiser, 1982.*

Kaplan, Aryeh. *Sefer Yetzirah: The Book of Creation. Weiser Books, 1997.*

Kushner, Lawrence. *The Book of Letters: A Mystical Hebrew Alphabet. Jewish Lights Publishing, 1990.*

Munk, Michael L. *The Wisdom in the Hebrew Alphabet. Mesorah Publications, 1983.*

Patai, Raphael. *The Hebrew Goddess. Wayne State University Press, 1990.*

Regardie, Israel. *The Tree of Life: A Study in Magic. Weiser Books, 2000.*

Samuel, Gabriella. *The Kabbalah Handbook: A Concise Encyclopedia of Terms and Concepts in Jewish Mysticism. TarcherPerigee, 2007.*

Scherman, Nosson. *The Complete ArtScroll Siddur. Mesorah Publications, 1984.*

Steinsaltz, Adin. *The Thirteen Petalled Rose: A Discourse on the Essence of Jewish Existence and Belief. Basic Books, 1991.*

Unterman, Alan (ed.). *The Kabbalistic Tradition: An Anthology of Jewish Mysticism. Penguin Classics, 2008.*

Z'ev ben Shimon Halevi. *Kabbalah and Exodus. Samuel Weiser, 1987.*

Penczak, Christopher. *The Mystical Foundation. Llewellyn Publishing, 2016.*

Glazerson, Matityahu. *Building Blocks of the Soul. Aronson Publishing, 1997.*

ChatGPT by OpenAI. *Language Model. Accessed [2024]. The primary use of this tool was to refine the content in this book through content editing. It accomplished this by offering detailed explanations and providing suggestions for various sections.*

Blumenthal, David R. (ed.). *Understanding Jewish Mysticism: A Source Reader. KTAV Publishing House, 1978.*

Hamilton-Parker, Craig. *The Hidden Meaning of Dreams. Sterling Publishing, 1999.*

Idel, Moshe. The Golem: *Jewish Magical and Mystical Traditions on the Artificial Anthropoid. SUNY Press, 1990.*

Matt, Daniel C. *The Essential Kabbalah: The Heart of Jewish Mysticism. HarperOne, 1995.*

Savedow, Steve (trans.). *The Sepher Rezial Hemelach: The Book of the Angel Rezial. Weiser Books, 2000.*

Nelson, Thomas (ed.). *King James Version of the Bible. Thomas Nelson, 1987.*

Strong, James. *Strong's Exhaustive Concordance of the Bible. Abingdon Press, 1890.*

Onions, C.T. *The Oxford Dictionary of English Etymology. Oxford University Press, 1966.*

Berg, Philip S. *Power of the Aleph-Bet. The Kabbalah Centre, 2009.*

Cohen, Martin S. *The Shaping of Jewish History: A Radical New Interpretation. UPA, 1999.*

Scholem, Gershom. *Major Trends in Jewish Mysticism. Schocken Books, 1995.*

Heschel, Abraham Joshua. *God in Search of Man: A Philosophy of Judaism. Farrar, Straus and Giroux, 1955.*

Wolfson, Elliot R. *Through a Speculum That Shines: Vision and Imagination in Medieval Jewish Mysticism. Princeton University Press, 1994.*

Grossman, Allen. *The Long Schoolroom: Lessons in the Bitter Logic of the Poetic Principle. University of Michigan Press, 1997.*

Goodman, Lenn E. *God of Abraham. Oxford University Press, 1996.*

Disclaimer
EDUCATIONAL PURPOSES

This book, "The Language of God Yahweh: Aleph to Tav - A Beginner's Guide to the Hebrew Letters," is intended for educational purposes only. The information provided herein, including the descriptions, interpretations, and meditations associated with the Hebrew Aleph-Beth, is meant to enhance understanding and appreciation of the Hebrew language, its spiritual significance, and its historical context.

The meditations and exercises included in this book are designed to facilitate personal reflection and spiritual growth. They are offered as suggestions and should be practiced with mindfulness and care. The author and publisher do not claim any medical, psychological, or therapeutic benefits from these practices.

Readers are encouraged to seek professional advice where appropriate and to use their discretion when engaging in any meditative practices. The content of this book is based on the author's research and interpretation and should not be considered definitive or exhaustive.

Readers are encouraged to conduct their own research into the specific Hebrew letters and meditations that best suit their personal journey.

KOS Books

To learn about - The Kingdom of Shalom

Visit www.kingdomof shalom.com